FROM THE LIBRARY OF

TCS & STARQUEST EXPEDITIONS

Machu Picchu

Machu Picchu
Exploring an Ancient Sacred Center

Johan Reinhard

FOURTH REVISED EDITION

COTSEN INSTITUTE OF ARCHAEOLOGY
UNIVERSITY OF CALIFORNIA, LOS ANGELES

This book is set in 10-point Adobe Garamond Pro, with titles in 35-point Helvetica Neue Ultra Light Extended
Edited by Joe Abbott
Designed by William Morosi
Index by Robert and Cynthia Swanson

Library of Congress Cataloging-in-Publication Data
Reinhard, Johan.
 Machu Picchu : exploring an ancient sacred center / Johan Reinhard. -- 4th rev. ed.
   p. cm. -- (World heritage and monument series ; 1)
 Includes bibliographical references and index.
 ISBN 978-1-931745-44-4 (pbk. : alk. paper)
 1. Machu Picchu Site (Peru) 2. Incas--Religion. 3. Inca architecture. 4. Incas--Antiquities. I. Cotsen Institute of Archaeology at UCLA. II. Title. III. Series.

 F3429.1.M3.R44 2007
 985'.019--dc22

2007022742

To the memories of
John Hyslop, Craig Morris, and Robert Randall—
Andean scholars and friends, who made invaluable contributions
to increasing our understanding of the Incas.

Contents

Prologue to the Fourth Edition

When I first began writing down my thoughts about Machu Picchu in the 1980s, I intended to publish them in an academic journal. During discussions with colleagues in Peru, however, I came to realize that they could be of interest to a broader public. Thus I decided to make the material available in a publication that would be more accessible yet still maintain elements crucial to a scientific approach, such as endnotes and references. Nonetheless, I should emphasize that this book is not intended as a substitute for volumes that provide details about the discovery of Machu Picchu, much less an in-depth overview of Inca culture.

Rather than a guidebook or a history of the ruins, this book presents a theory that attempts to explain the meaning of Machu Picchu and the reasons why it was built in such a dramatic location. This pursuit leads to a reexamination of the possible significance of some of the site's key architectural features. Despite the book's somewhat academic approach and its limited distribution in Peru, I have been agreeably surprised at how widely it has come to be read. I am pleased to be able to reissue it in this North American edition, with a few additions to bring it up to date.

Peruvian and Argentine archaeologists working at an Inca site on the summit of Llullaillaco (6,739 m/22,109 feet).

Although I have spent fifteen years conducting research in the Andes since the publication of the first edition in 1991, I have found little that needs changing regarding the facts and theory originally presented. (Indeed, as the reader will discover, there has been new information that has appeared to support it.) I have, however, included an epilogue in order to summarize theoretical approaches and recent archaeological discoveries in the region and to place my interpretation of Machu Picchu in the context of a larger theory about sacred landscape in the Andes.

Few Inca artifacts of importance have been recovered from the ruins of Machu Picchu since this book first appeared, but several have been found elsewhere. These have helped to increase our understanding of Inca culture and especially of their ceremonial sites and the rituals and offerings made at them. In my own case, during the 1990s I participated in discoveries of frozen Inca mummies and artifacts on mountains as high as 22,100 feet in Argentina and southern Peru. I was also involved in underwater archaeological expeditions in Lake Titicaca, one of the most sacred places in the Inca Empire, and undertook investigations of some little-known Inca ceremonial centers of special significance in Inca religion, including the temples of Vilcanota, Ancocagua, and Coropuna.

The results of this research provided dramatic evidence of the importance of sacred landscape to the Incas and thus underscored the need for the theoretical approach I have taken in this book. Although there may never be final answers to some questions about Machu Picchu, we can certainly come to a better understanding of it by looking at this magnificent site as it would have been seen through the eyes of the Incas.

Johan Reinhard
Franklin, West Virginia
April 2007

Acknowledgments

My research on sacred geography in the Cuzco and Machu Picchu region has involved numerous visits since 1981. The organizations that supplied the principal financing for this research were Rolex Montres, the Organization of American States, the National Geographic Society, the Social Science Research Council, and the National Endowment for the Humanities. I would like to express my gratitude to these organizations for their kind support.

It would be impossible to name all the individuals who in one way or another have contributed to the project over more than a decade. The following people were especially helpful and they have my warm thanks: Trinidad Aguilar, Catherine Allen, Moises Aragon, Carmen Araoz, Constance Ayala-Parrish, Jim Bartle, Richard Bielefeldt, Elena Bravo, Joanna Burkhardt, Luciano Carbajal, Jesus Contreras, Jean Jacques Decoster, Jorge Flores, Peter Frost, Peter Getzels, Gerard Geurten, Harriet Gordon, Maarten van de Guchte, Federico Kauffmann-Doig, Ann Kendall, Peter Lewis, Patricia Lyon, Gordon McEwan, Frank Meddens, Carlos Milla, Max Milligan, Alberto Miori, Juan Victor Nuñez del Prado, Italo Oberti, Vilma Olivera, Jean Pierre Protzen, Cirilo Pumayalhi, Americo Rivas, Maria Rostworowski, John Rowe, Washington Rozas, Wolfgang Schuler, Jeannette Sherbondy, Gary Urton, Alfredo Valencia, Roger Valencia, Ruben Velarde, Benito Waman, Wendy Weeks, and Gary Ziegler. A preliminary draft of the first edition benefited from suggestions made by John Carlson, David Dearborn, Adriana von Hagen, John Hyslop, Margaret MacLean, Robert Randall, and Tom Zuidema. I would like particularly to thank David Dearborn for supplying me with the major star azimuths on the horizon as seen from the Intihuatana, Kenneth Wright for allowing use of his map of the Machu Picchu ruins, Vince Lee for his reconstructions of sites in Vilcabamba, Margaret MacLean for the use of her plans of sites along the Inca Trail, and Gary Ziegler for permitting my publishing a plan showing alignments between Machu Picchu and Llaktapata.

Research in the Department of Cuzco was greatly facilitated by past directors of the National Institute of Culture: Fernín Dias, Gustavo Manrique, Oscar Nuñez del Prado, and Danilo Pallardel. Several members of the institute assisted in the research, and I owe special thanks to Percy Ardiles, Arminda Gibaja, Fidel Ramos, Wilbert San Roman, Leoncio Vera, and Wilfredo Yepez. I am indebted to Fernando Astete and Ruben Orellana of the Archaeology Survey Office within the institute for kindly sharing with me the unpublished results of their extensive field surveys and for organizing and participating in an expedition to Cerro San Miguel. Luis Barreda and Manuel Chavez graciously made available their personal libraries.

Alfredo Valencia was generous in explaining much of the recent work with which he has been involved at the site. Tom Hendrickson of Peruvian Andean Treks and Alfredo Ferreyros of Explorandes were very helpful both with information and in organizing expeditions undertaken in the region. The South American Explorers provided valuable support in several ways. Robert von Kaupp, Vince Lee, and Stuart White kindly assisted me with investigations in the Vilcabamba, and Robert also generously gave me copies of his numerous, detailed reports. I would like to thank Bell Canada, Eagle Creek, Marmot, North Face, Patagonia, Recreational Equipment, and Timberland for donations of equipment. I am deeply grateful to Joseph and Sharon Richardson for generously supporting research undertaken to the west of Machu Picchu.

Finally, I owe a special thanks to Alfredo Ferreyros, past president of the Instituto Machu Picchu, for making possible the second edition and for kindly writing the introduction to this fourth edition. Of course, I am solely responsible for any factual errors that might have occurred in the text.

Introduction

The fourth (and first North American) edition of *Machu Picchu: The Sacred Center* contains numerous additions to the illustrations, along with a revised text and bibliography, which together make it an invaluable resource. The book presents an interpretation of Machu Picchu based on two new fields of research known as "high-altitude archaeology" (requiring mountaineering skills) and "landscape archaeology" (the placement of ruins within the larger landscapes of which they are a part). In the Andes Dr. Reinhard is a pioneer in these fields and their most renowned practitioner.

This edition, enriched by recent discoveries, is presented in an easy-to-read format. The author's perspective is based on his research over several years in the region, and the text is supplemented by an epilogue, appendix, endnotes, and bibliography to which the reader can refer for further information. This enables the work to be both accessible and scholarly, building on multidisciplinary investigations carried out by foreign and Peruvian scholars over the past decades.

Dr. Reinhard establishes the importance of Machu Picchu based on its location—part of a network of sites joined by Inca trails of varied importance embodied in this unique topography. The site lies at the center of an impressive landscape, much of which is now part of a National Protected Area established by the Peruvian Government—the Machu Picchu Historical Sanctuary (MPHS). By reading this book, we are able to comprehend the profound understanding the Incas had of the importance of their natural resources, the cycles of nature, and the ecological component of day-to-day life.

No one really knows why Machu Picchu and adjoining sites were abandoned by the Incas before the arrival of the Spanish conquistadors. But we can suppose, in part based on photographs since its rediscovery by Hiram Bingham, that the ecosystems present today in the MPHS were utilized somewhat differently by the Incas. Agro-ecological practices utilizing Andean land-use patterns were established by the Incas, thereby permitting human activity and settlements in this rugged region.

For all those wanting to enrich their knowledge of the MPHS, this book is a must. It is an honor to be able to introduce this book, which adds significantly to the fount of knowledge and information we have of this site and of the region in general.

Alfredo E. Ferreyros
Executive Director of Conservation International, Peru
Former President of the Instituto Machu Picchu
Cuzco, Peru

Machu Picchu

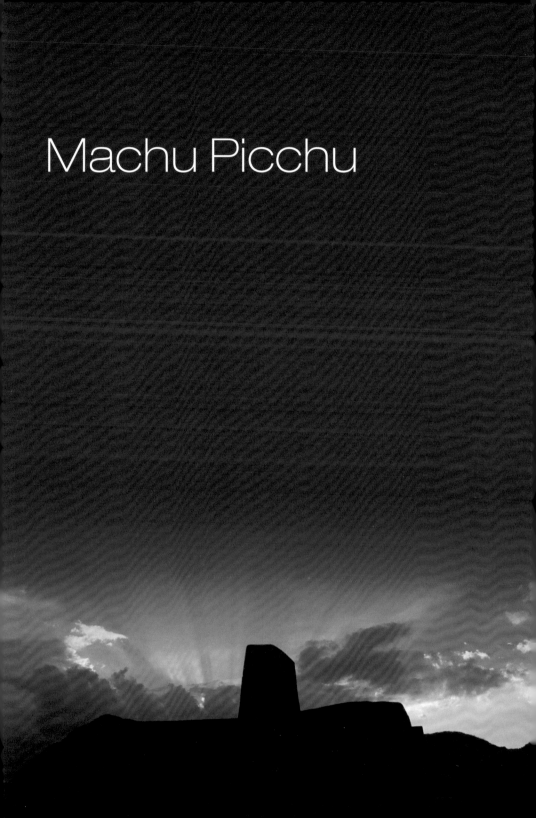

The Incas and the Discovery of Machu Picchu

Figure 1.1. The classic view of Machu Picchu with the mountain Huayna Picchu in the background.

Figure 1.2. Machu Picchu as seen with a telephoto lens from the Inca Trail at Inti Punku (the "sun gate").

THE INCAS

My first view of Machu Picchu seemed like something from a dream—an ancient city materializing out of the clouds. After four days of hiking the Inca Trail, I had reached a pass where Machu Picchu became visible with rugged peaks surrounding it in the background. I thought I knew what to expect, but Machu Picchu is that way—it is one of the few places in the world where reality can surpass one's imagination. The Incas managed to construct a site that never ceases to astonish, even after repeated visits (Figures 1.1 and 1.2).

Machu Picchu, however, is only one of the many achievements of the Incas, who forged an empire that was the largest to exist in the prehispanic Americas (Figure 1.3). The Incas dominated South America when the Spaniards arrived in AD 1532, having conquered a region extending from northern Ecuador to central Chile and totaling more than 2,500 miles in length. Since the focus of this book is on interpreting Machu Picchu, in this chapter I will provide only a brief summary about its discovery and the extraordinary culture of the Incas. The reader should refer to some of the fine publications on these topics for more information. (1)

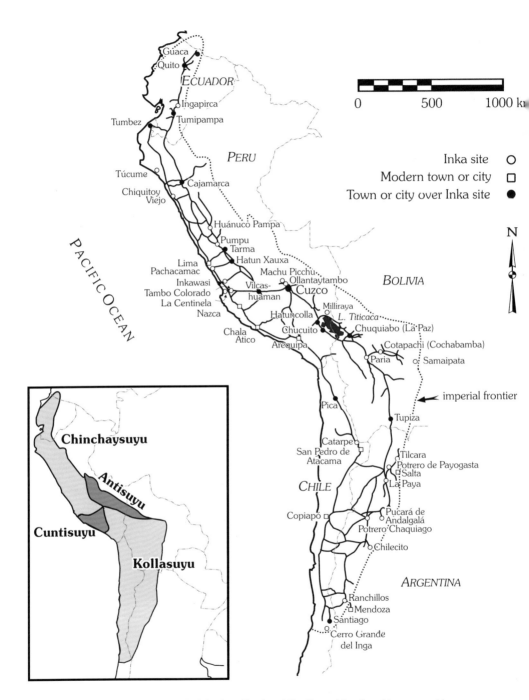

Figure 1.3. Map showing the extend of the Inca Empire at the time of the Spanish conquest in AD 1532 (from D'Altroy 2002).

As important as the Inca culture came to be, it was only the last in a long line of civilizations that arose in the Andean region over the previous three millennia. Archaeologists divide the central Andes into time periods called "horizons" (when a particular art style was found extending over a broad area) and "intermediate periods" (when widespread art styles were absent). The Early Horizon (ca. 1200–200 BC) was associated with the Chavin art style, which spread over a large area of central coastal Peru and the highlands. Regional art styles characterized the Early Intermediate Period (ca. 200 BC–AD 600), with the Nazca and Moche being the best known. The Middle Horizon (ca. AD 600–1000) was established based on the Tiahuanaco-Huari art style that extended from the southern highlands to the north coast of Peru. During the Late Intermediate Period (ca. AD 1000–1475) regional art styles again arose over limited areas, with the Chimu culture holding sway along the north coast of Peru.

Although the Incas dominated the Late Horizon (ca. AD 1475–1535), which lasted until the Spanish conquest, many aspects of their empire had origins in institutions and technologies that had developed long before it arose to prominence, especially during the Middle Horizon. (2) Nonetheless, the Incas accomplished astounding feats of their own, and many of these took place less than a century before the arrival of the Spaniards.

One of the best-known examples of these is the Inca road system, which was one of the most extensive ever built in the ancient world, rivaling that of the Roman Empire. It has been estimated that the Incas built as much as 20,000 miles of roads. The Incas did not have the wheel, but their road system and llama caravans allowed for products to be transported throughout the empire. All of this took place in one of the most rugged terrains on Earth.

The Incas began to expand out of the region of Cuzco, capital of their empire, sometime around AD 1438. The emperor Pachacuti (ca. AD 1438–1463) undertook campaigns that soon brought a vast area of the central Andes under Inca control. The period of Pachacuti's reign is the first for which we have unambiguous historical and archaeological evidence. It marked the beginning of major building initiatives, including such well-known sites as Machu Picchu. Inca stonemasons became famous for fitting together multi-ton stones without mortar—and so well that a knife blade could not be slid between them (cf. Figures 1.4 and 1.5).

Pachacuti reputedly also began the conceptual organization of the empire (Tawantinsuyu) into four (*tawantin*) parts (*suyus*), with Cuzco at its center. In Cuzco an elaborate series of imaginary lines (*ceques*) was projected onto the immediate landscape. More than 300 sacred sites, mostly associated with natural features of the landscape, were linked by the lines that mostly originated in or near the Temple of the Sun and extended outward in a radiating pattern, thereby creating what became known as the *ceque* system.

Figure 1.4. Aerial view of the Inca fortress and ceremonial complex of Sacsahuaman, which overlooks Cuzco. Walls involved the fitting of cut stones, many weighing more than 30 tons.

Pachacuti's son, Tupac Yupanqui (Topa Inca, ca. AD 1463–1493), conquered more lands, until the borders reached from modern-day Ecuador to central Chile. The limits of the empire were reached during the reign of Topa Inca's son Huayna Capac (ca. AD 1493–1525). His death was followed by a conflict between his sons over his successor. The struggle resulted in a weakened empire at the time the Spaniards arrived in Peru. Taking advantage of this division (along with their superior armor, the dissatisfaction of some tribes against Inca rule, and the after-effects of an epidemic), the Spaniards were able to conquer a state that rivaled any in Europe in size and riches.

The administration of such an extensive multi-ethnic state was itself a major feat, made possible by initiatives that incorporated conquered groups into a highly integrated economic, political, and religious system. Deities were believed to control the success of crops and herds, of wars, of illnesses, of business transactions, and so forth. Everything was intertwined.

The Incas helped ensure their control of the state through several means, including the establishment of a single language, Quechua, as a principal means of communication. They built a system of posts or way stations (*tambos*) to accommodate travelers and to hold supplies, and runners (*chasquis*) were used for the rapid transmission of messages.

Figure 1.5. Fine Inca stonework in a wall in Cuzco.

Figure 1.6. Inca terracing near the town of Ollantaytambo in the Sacred Valley.

The Incas became especially associated with the spread of irrigation and maize agriculture throughout their empire. In broad terms there are two types of agriculture in the Andes. One is based on highland staple root crops, principally the potato, which can be grown at elevations up to 16,400 feet in some parts of the Andes. Other highland crops include grain foods, such as quinoa, the world's most nutritious cereal. The second type of agriculture takes place in the lower elevations and has evolved around maize. Although irrigation and fertilizers are usually necessary for a successful crop, there is no need to leave land fallow, and the grain can be stored for long periods—a major plus for feeding an army.

To better control and develop the regions they conquered, the Incas moved entire communities (*mitimaes*) to colonize them, thereby insuring local support groups and promoting integration. They supported local shrines, while keeping some of the main idols of the conquered peoples as virtual hostages in Cuzco. The Incas undertook major public works throughout their empire, such as terracing, irrigation, and storehouses, in order to offset any food shortages (see Figure 1.6). They also promoted the expansion of herding into new areas and set up systems for the redistribution of products and services.

No documents predate the arrival of the Spaniards because the Andean peoples lacked writing. They developed an elaborate system of record keeping, however, by using variations of knots and colors on cords called *quipus* (Figure 1.7). The Incas' organizational and logistical ability set their empire apart from any that had come before. This ability also enabled them to undertake a systematic campaign to climb to the summits of the highest peaks in the Americas—mountains that were often revered as the most important deities of the peoples the Incas conquered. In addition to mountains, many other parts of the landscape were venerated, making for what has come to be called a "sacred geography." The Incas had a precise knowledge of topography and were able to make models of the areas they conquered that lay even at the extremes of their empire. One such model of the larger Cuzco region was so well done that the chronicler Garcilaso de la Vega wrote in the early 1600s that "the best cosmographer in the world could not have done it better."[1]

Inca religion shared many fundamental concepts held by other ethnic groups throughout the Andes. They all worshipped their ancestors and features of the landscape, and this practice was clearly widespread long before the Incas and

Figure 1.7. A *quipu*, a set of knotted strings that the Incas used for record keeping.

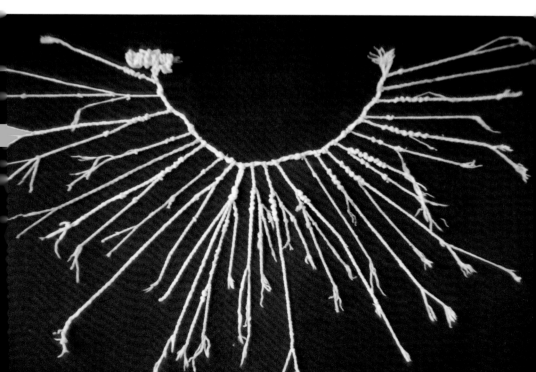

well outside their empire. Although the Incas also worshipped a large number of supernatural beings, especially important in their state religious pantheon were Inti (the sun), Illapa (the weather god), and Viracocha (the creator). Many legends exist about Viracocha, but a common one has him rising from Lake Titicaca and then beginning his creative acts (Figure 1.8). Several other deities of great regional significance, such as Pachacamac, Catequil, Pariacaca, and Coropuna, were also associated with creative acts.

The Inca emperor was not only a secular ruler but also head of Inca state religion, which was imposed throughout the lands the Incas conquered. (3) The Incas claimed to be directly descended from Inti. Interestingly, the evidence from history, ethnography, and archaeology supports the conclusion that sun worship was *not* of major importance throughout much of the Andes prior to the Inca conquest. The sun may have become significant as an Inca state deity because it was visible to everyone. Deities of the local landscape were of greater importance to indigenous groups prior to their being conquered by the Incas. Indeed, the Incas continued to allow—and often even supported—their worship, as long as the people accepted sun worship into their religious activities.

Illapa, the Incas' weather deity, was of widespread importance because of his control of meteorological phenomena—lightning, thunder, snow, hail, storms, and rain—and thus the fertility of plants and animals. He was reportedly the most widely worshipped of the state deities and only slightly less important than the sun. It seems likely that the belief in a generalized weather god arose, at least in part, out of an attempt on the part of the Incas to bring numerous weather and mountain deities under one unified concept. As we will see, local weather deities and mountain gods were widely perceived as being the same.

Besides Inti, Illapa, and Viracocha, other deities in Inca religion played key roles with regard to fertility, such as Mamacocha (the ocean) and Pachamama (Earth Mother), who was widely worshipped and still is today. In addition to the sun and the moon (Inti's consort), many astronomical phenomena were revered, including certain constellations and the Milky Way. Aside from mountains, other landscape features, such as lakes, rivers, springs, and unusual rock formations, were often worshipped for fertility. Traditional religion throughout the Andes continues to focus on nature spirits associated with fertility up to the present day—including in the region of Machu Picchu, as we will see.

Figure 1.8. Island of the Sun in Lake Titicaca, legendary place of origin of the Incas.

THE DISCOVERY OF MACHU PICCHU

Machu Picchu is the best-known archaeological site in South America—and for good reason. It is located in one of the most spectacular settings in the Andes, set amidst lush tropical vegetation on a ridge overlooking a winding river hundreds of meters below and with views toward snowcapped mountains (Figure 1.9). In addition, Machu Picchu is one of the few Inca sites to remain relatively intact and contains some of the finest structures built in pre-Columbian times. It thus allows us a rare opportunity to study its buildings almost as they were at the time they were abandoned. And since so many surrounding sites are also well preserved, we can examine Machu Picchu within the larger system of which it played such a critical part (Figure 1.10).

Nowhere, however, do the earliest Spanish writers describe the site, and there are no descendants of the original inhabitants of the area who might be able to explain its meaning. Indeed, Machu Picchu's existence was not even revealed to the outside world until after Hiram Bingham's visit in 1911. Bingham had organized an expedition to search for the last Inca capital of Vilcabamba, the location of which had become lost in the centuries following the Spaniards' destruction of the site in the 1570s.

An explorer and historian, Bingham had already traveled in the Andes previously, even having reached Choquequirao, a site to the south of Machu Picchu that some had believed was the legendary Vilcabamba (Figure 1.11). After receiving the backing of Yale University, in 1911 he led a group down the Urubamba River along a route that had been opened up only a few years earlier in order to help increase trade between the highlands and the lower, forested region. Before long, it would become the route taken by the railway and the principal way used by visitors to reach Machu Picchu up to the present day.

Advised of ruins on a ridge above the river, Bingham climbed up to them with his military escort and a local farmer to "discover" Machu Picchu. In fact, the name *Picho* (i.e., *picchu* or "peak") had been noted in documents in the 1550s and 1700s, and a few people had already been aware of the ruins prior to 1911. It was Bingham, however, who surveyed the site and made it known to the larger public, and he has been rightly credited with being the "scientific discoverer" of Machu Picchu.

Having found the ruins so early in his expedition, he spent little time there and instead continued with his search for more ruins. He located such important sites as Vitcos and Espiritu Pampa (which turned out to be the original Vilcabamba—unbeknownst to Bingham). Although an initial mapping of Machu Picchu was completed by two members of Bingham's team in 1911, the site

Figure 1.9. Machu Picchu is located near the lower end of a long ridge that descends from Nevado Salcantay.

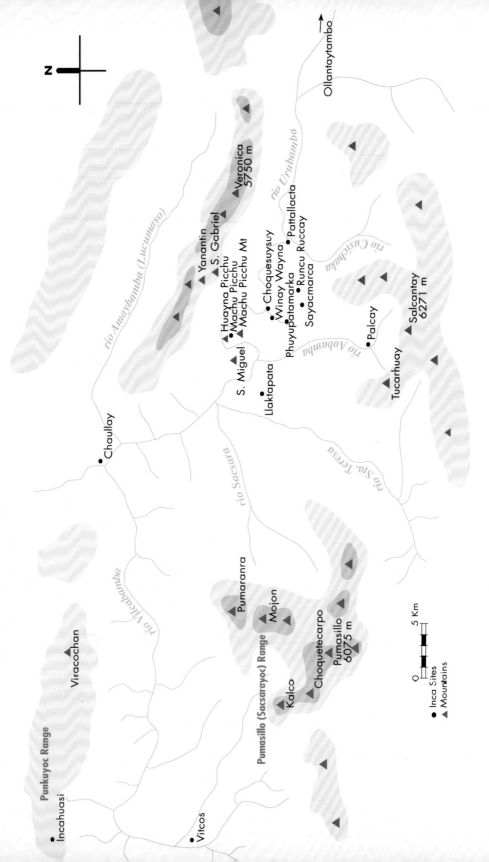

Figure 1.10. The wider region in which Machu Picchu is situated. Rivers, mountains, and Inca sites referred to in the text are noted.

was mainly cleared, surveyed, photographed, and excavated during Bingham's second expedition of 1912. He came to believe that Machu Picchu was both the Vilcabamba of the Incas and their place of origin. The results of his work were published by the National Geographic Society in 1913, bringing instant fame to the site.

Bingham returned in 1915 and found yet more ruins, including most of those that lie along the now famous Inca Trail. For a number of reasons, he did not return to Machu Picchu until 1948, when the road from the river to the site was opened. (4) In 1981 the Machu Picchu Historical Sanctuary was established, with its boundaries set to include, and protect, a larger ecological zone (Figure 1.12).

Despite its renown, there has always been an air of mystery about Machu Picchu, and it continues to excite the imaginations of visitors. Scholars have long struggled to answer some of the most basic questions: Why was Machu Picchu built in such an inaccessible location? Why was it abandoned? What was its meaning?

Many attempts have been made to answer these questions, some based on careful scholarship, others on speculations unburdened by facts. In this book I am

Figure 1.11. The ruins of Choquequirao with mountains of the Vilcabamba behind.

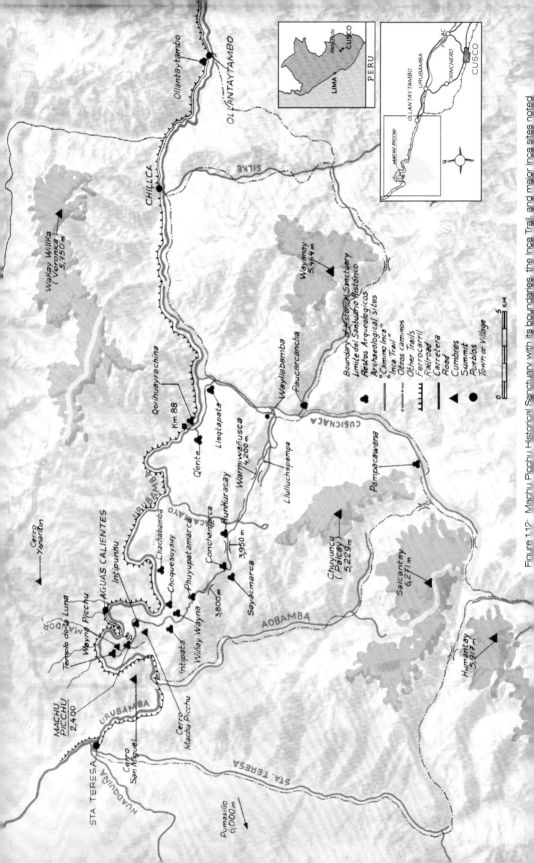

FIGURE 1.12: Machu Picchu Historical Sanctuary with its boundaries, the Inca Trail, and major Inca sites noted

concerned with examining Machu Picchu in relation to the sacred geographical beliefs of the Incas. Such an approach has proven useful in examining pre-Inca ceremonial centers elsewhere in the Andes,[2] and the importance of geographical features in Inca religion has been amply demonstrated.[3] Although Machu Picchu was more than just a religious center, as we will see below, it had many structures of finely worked stone. Based on what the Spaniards wrote about other Inca sites, we know that these buildings were of ritual significance, and Bingham named many of them with this in mind. Thus guidebooks list names such as the Principal Temple, the Intihuatana, the Temple of the Moon, the Priest's House, and the Temple of Three Windows. There is no doubt that the religious aspect of the site was a dominant one.[4] The archaeologists John Rowe and Luis Valcárcel have pointed out its religious importance and noted how a combination of geographical features found at, and near, its location would have been of significance to the Incas.[5] It is this combination of features, alluded to only briefly by these scholars, that I will examine here.

Given the lack of information about the Machu Picchu region and the few written documents about it dating back to Colonial times, it is necessary to utilize information on Inca beliefs from adjacent areas, along with an examination of the archaeological remains and current-day beliefs in the surrounding region and near Cuzco, heart of the Inca Empire. Unfortunately, there is little information available about some key parts of the landscape. This deficiency requires that we pull together diverse pieces to provide a coherent picture of what the situation was probably like during the Inca presence at Machu Picchu. Although incomplete, the data are consistent with the general pattern of beliefs that existed during the Inca period.

I intend to show that Machu Picchu can be better understood when analyzed within the context of the surrounding geographical features and their association with astronomical events considered sacred by the Incas. The methodology employed here to help establish this premise relies not only on the use of Inca beliefs and customs but also on a study of the natural landscape and present-day beliefs with roots in Inca concepts. This does not mean that such beliefs have remained unchanged, only that in broad terms they reflect a view of the environment in accordance with that held by the Incas. They can, therefore, help in the development of a theory that better explains the known facts about Machu Picchu. Assuming that the theory is capable of providing a reasonable explanation for the site's location, it follows that it can in turn assist in the interpretation of Machu Picchu's function and of the meanings of some of its principal features. It is time now to examine the sacred geography surrounding the ruins of Machu Picchu.

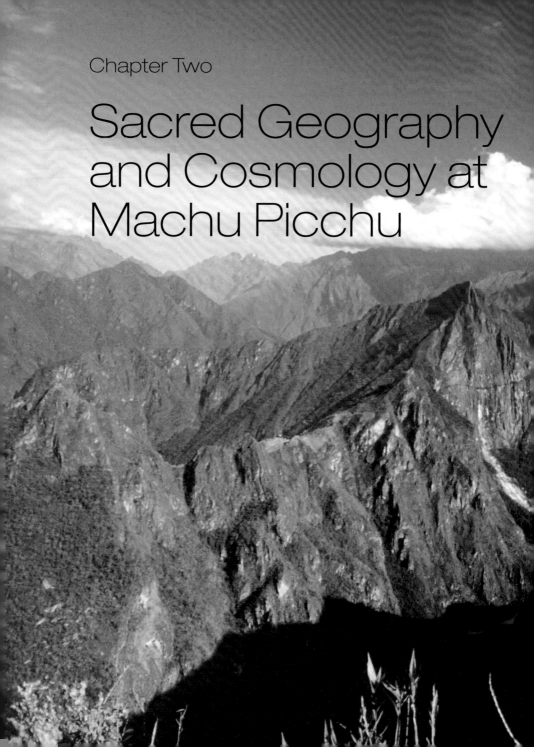

Chapter Two

Sacred Geography and Cosmology at Machu Picchu

Figure 2.1a. A view from the San Miguel ridge with Machu Picchu visible at the lower left and Salcantay to the upper right.

Figure 2.1b. Panorama of the Sanctuary from San Miguel Mountain.

Panorama of the Sanctuary
from San Miguel Mountain

Salcantay

Aobamba Valley

Phuyupatamarca

Machu Picchu Mtn.

Inca Trail

Inca Bridge

Urubamba River

Inca Trail

Intipunku

Urubamba River

CUSCO

Machu Picchu

Wayna Picchu

Temple of
the Moon

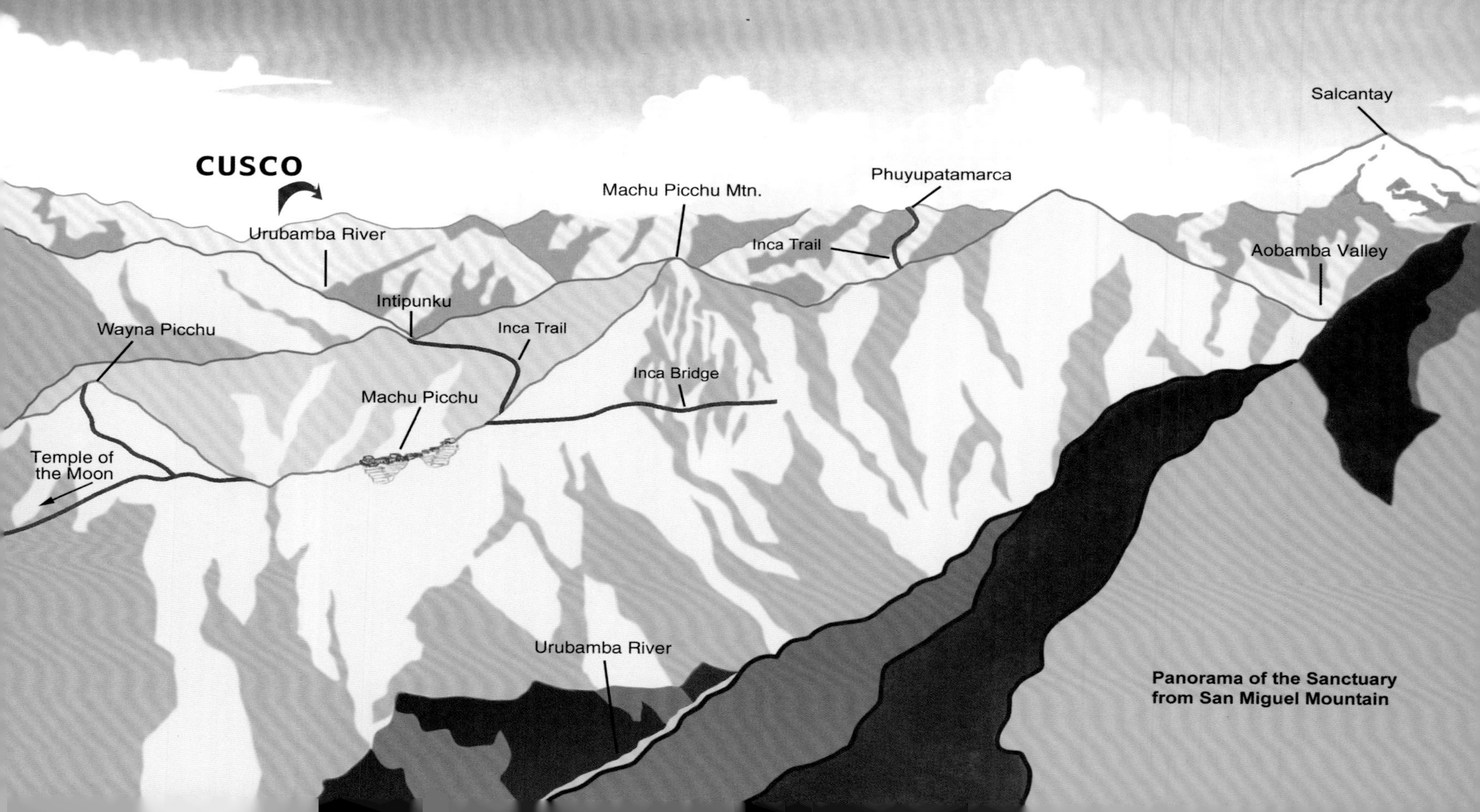

SACRED GEOGRAPHY

The term *sacred geography* refers to the geographical features (mountains, rivers, lakes, boulders, caves, springs) believed to possess supernatural powers or to be the embodiments of supernatural beings. In the Andes the high mountains (commonly called *apus* in the Cuzco region) were (and still are) considered among the most powerful of the traditional deities. Lakes were also important but do not seem to have played a major role in the region of Machu Picchu, where the lakes are small and widely scattered. Rivers, especially the Urubamba (Vilcanota) River, springs, caves, and boulders all played roles in the sacred geography of the region, but it is the rugged mountain topography surrounding Machu Picchu that appears to have been of primary importance. Before attempting to interpret the meaning of Machu Picchu, it is necessary to examine some of the past and current-day beliefs relating to this topography.

SALCANTAY AND AUSANGATE

Rising in solitary splendor due south of Machu Picchu, Salcantay (6,271 m/20,574 feet) is one of the highest and most impressive mountains in the Department of Cuzco, and it dominates the region of Machu Picchu (Figures 2.1 and 2.2). Visible from great distances, it was highly revered in Inca times and continues to be so today. The name *Salcantay* probably stems from the Quechua word *salcca* (*salqa*), which means "wild or uncivilized."[6]

Traditional people living near Cuzco perceive Salcantay as the "brother" of Ausangate.[7] Ausangate (6,372 m/20,905 feet) is the highest mountain in the Department of Cuzco and the only snowcapped mountain visible from the city of Cuzco (Figures 2.3 and 2.4). Many people believe the two mountains to be the "fathers" of all the mountains and to be equally powerful.[8] During my study I found that these mountains were often the first to be named in rituals in the Cuzco region, and their permission is frequently sought before making offerings to the other mountains.[9] When such offerings are made by local communities, they generally revolve around requests for good weather and increased crop and livestock fertility.[10] When done on the behalf of individuals, the requests are often concerned with health, theft, loss of items, desires for increased prosperity, or success in business.[11]

Salcantay's importance is not restricted to the area around the city of Cuzco. The anthropologist Juan Nuñez del Prado found it to be a principal mountain deity

Figure 2.2. Salcantay as seen with a telephoto lens from the platform above Phuyupatamarka.

for the entire Department of Cuzco and a tutelary deity for the Department of Apurimac as well.[12] One of the earliest references to Salcantay is that of the Spanish priest Cristóbal de Albornoz, who wrote in 1583 that Salcantay was "very revered."[13] Another early source, Juan de Santa Cruz Pachacuti, wrote that "Sallcatay" was one of the mountains to which the "huacas" (sacred places or objects, here referring to various deities) were banished by the god Tonopa (Tunupa).[14] In a document of 1697 found in the Cuzco Archives, Salcantay was one of the principal mountain deities called upon for curing a man in Cuzco.[15] Salcantay is still commonly invoked in rituals to cure illnesses in the Cuzco region.[16]

In the late 1800s Salcantay was noted as being a male (called Urco Salcantay) (*urco* meaning male or mountain) and his wife was Huaca (or Huacay) Huillca (Waqaywillka or Veronica) (see below), also called China Salcantay (*china* meaning female).[17] Interestingly, these names have also been used for the two summits of Salcantay: China Salcantay as the female and Urco Salcantay as the male.[18]

Two summits are both believed to be irascible deities quick to avenge themselves on anyone who disturbs them. Salcantay's wrath was also noted near Cuzco and further emphasized by a ritual specialist, Luciano Carbajal, in Ollantaytambo.[19] This serves to demonstrate the fear this deity arouses in people and the power attributed to him. It is no surprise to find that people crossing the range near Salcantay still make simple offerings in order to avoid his wrath (Figure 2.5).

In the Cuzco region many ritual specialists (*paqos* and *altomisayoqs*) consider themselves under the domain of either Salcantay or Ausangate, depending on where they resided when they learned their trade.[20] In order to be "presented" to these mountains, the student and his teacher should journey to their slopes.[21] Ritual specialists from Quillabamba in the tropical lowlands are also said to go to Salcantay for spiritual empowerment.[22]

Some ritual specialists claim that initiations to Salcantay take place at lakes near the mountain Suparaura (south of Salcantay) or at lakes near Pumasillo (closer to and west of Salcantay).[23] Suparaura (5,106 m/16,752 feet) lies to the south of Abancay (southwest of Cuzco) and was noted as being a very important deity at the time of the Spanish conquest.[24] Albornoz, writing in the late 1500s, stated that it was the principal deity of the Aymaraes people who inhabited that region.[25] Because Suparaura is a much lower mountain and farther from Cuzco, we can assume that the Incas considered it less powerful than Salcantay, just as it is considered today.

Figure 2.3. The snowcapped mountain of Ausangate stands out to the east of Cuzco.

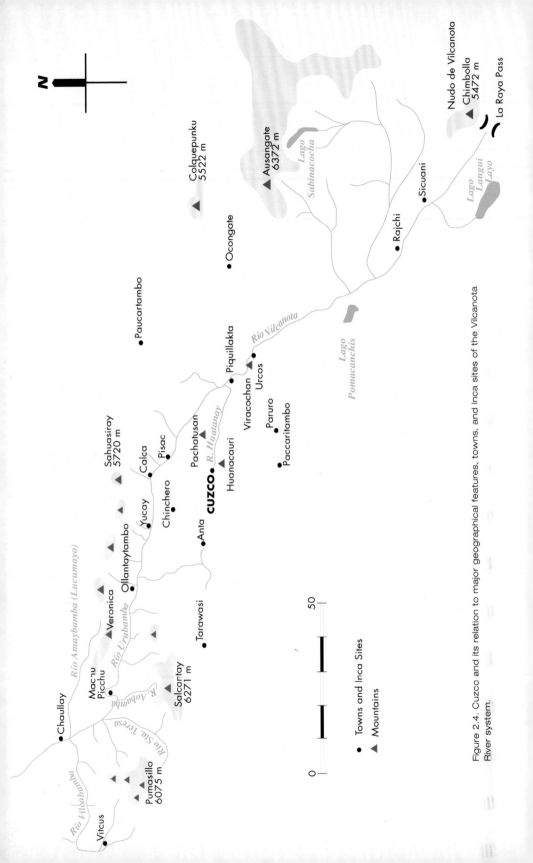

Figure 2.4. Cuzco and its relation to major geographical features, towns, and Inca sites of the Vilcanota River system.

Figure 2.5. A man from the Sacred Valley makes an offering of coca leaves to Salcantay while crossing a high pass.

The conceptualized dividing line between the domains of Salcantay and Ausangate is at Cuzco, with slight variations depending on where a given ritual specialist resides. For example, a *paqo* living in Huasao, 18 km east of Cuzco, might perceive Huasao as the place of division.[26] The majority of *paqos* interviewed in the region of Cuzco, however, placed the dividing line in the sacred capital of the Incas.

The Incas considered a mountain close to Cuzco, Huanacauri, to be one of the most sacred places in the empire (Figure 2.6). In current-day beliefs Huanacauri derives power from Ausangate and is still widely worshipped in the region. (5) The extent of Ausangate's power, however, was not limited to the Cuzco region. For example, one *paqo* claimed that Ausangate's domain extended all the way to Lake Titicaca, and an anthropologist noted that Ausangate is one of the most powerful mountain deities worshipped in the area bordering Lake Titicaca to the northwest.[27]

Not surprisingly, Ausangate and Salcantay are the highest mountains in the entire Department of Cuzco. It is necessary to go all the way to the Cordillera Real in Bolivia on the northeast side of Lake Titicaca to find a mountain higher than these two peaks to the southeast, and none is higher to the north. Only one, Coropuna,

Figure 2.6. A view over the central part of Cuzco with Huanacauri on the left skyline.

Figure 2.7. Modern-day offerings for mountain gods can include a llama fetus, colored threads, metallic figurines, sweets, and products from the ocean and the jungle lowlands.

is higher to the southwest of Cuzco, and this volcano is considerably distant. Aside from Coropuna, the only mountains higher in Peru are found in the Cordilleras Blanca and Huayhuash, far to the northwest. It is no coincidence that these higher mountains were also very important in Inca religious beliefs once the Incas had expanded their empire to include the regions in which they are located.[28]

Ausangate and Salcantay also constitute the highest mountains whose snows feed the rivers that flow into the jungle. In the region of Salcantay this deity is the one perceived as the "owner" of all products from the lowland forested area considered to be powerful, such as coca leaves, cane alcohol, coffee, and cacao.[29] Salcantay is renowned throughout the forested hills, including the provinces of La Convención, Calca, and Paucartambo to the north and east of Salcantay and the province of Anta to the south.[30] In the Cuzco region sacred power is associated with the tropical forest,[31] and several tropical plants are thought to contain magical properties and are used in rituals around Cuzco (see Figure 2.7).

It might be of interest here to note the association that Salcantay has with coca, a tropical plant of great significance in Inca ceremonies. Some writers, such as Eugenio Alarco and Carlos Troll, believe that Machu Picchu (which is dominated by Salcantay as we have seen) played a part in the cultivation and trading of coca leaves.[32] Recent discoveries of large areas of terracing near Machu Picchu and at the site itself support this theory. Although it is unclear whether coca was grown at Machu Picchu,[33] this uncertainty does not rule out the possibility that the site played a role in the coca leaf trade.

A document of 1568 noted that Indians cultivated coca in the valley below Machu Picchu.[34] Since in the early years of the conquest the Spaniards generally took over existing coca plantations that belonged to the Incas, this would indicate that coca was grown in the area during the period Machu Picchu was a functioning center. This seems even more likely given the isolation of the region, which bordered on territory controlled for years by rebel Incas unwilling to submit to the Spaniards, and its having been conquered by the Inca emperor Pachacuti, who began Inca expansion in this region in the mid-1400s.[35] The use of coca today is still invariably accompanied by invocations to the mountains,[36] including in the Vilcabamba region, where Machu Picchu is located.[37] In view of the beliefs noted above, Salcantay can be expected to have played an important religious-economic role not only with regard to coca but also with regard to other crops from the forested hills and lowlands.

COSMOLOGY AND SALCANTAY

There are also links between Salcantay and astronomical phenomena, especially stars in the Milky Way. Salcantay's association with the Southern Cross would not have gone unnoticed by the Incas at Machu Picchu. From Machu Picchu the Southern Cross is seen to rise on the east and to set on the west of Salcantay, and since it is above a point due south when it reaches its highest position in the sky,[38] it would also have been directly above Salcantay. Several scholars (e.g., the anthropologists Tom Zuidema and Gary Urton in 1976) have demonstrated the importance of the Southern Cross (and adjacent stars) and the Milky Way in Inca thought.[39] Information collected in the Cuzco region during recent years provides additional evidence for why this is so.

Urton described in his publications of 1978 and 1981 current-day beliefs in the Cuzco region with regard to the Quechua zodiac, the celestial plane of orientation that includes star groupings of the Milky Way. He noted that they are clearly

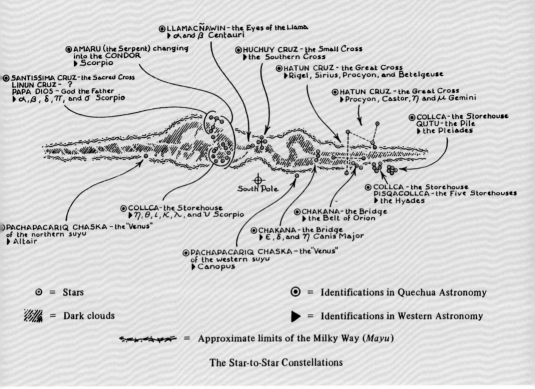

LLAMACÑAWIN - the Eyes of the Llama
▶ α and β Centauri

AMARU (the Serpent) changing
into the CONDOR
▶ Scorpio

HUCHUY CRUZ - the Small Cross
▶ the Southern Cross

SANTISSIMA CRUZ - the Sacred Cross
LINUN CRUZ - ?
PAPA DIOS - God the Father
▶ α, β, δ, π, and σ Scorpio

HATUN CRUZ - the Great Cross
▶ Rigel, Sirius, Procyon, and Betelgeuse

HATUN CRUZ - the Great Cross
▶ Procyon, Castor, η, and μ Gemini

COLLCA - the Storehouse
QUTU - the Pile
▶ the Pleiades

South Pole

COLLCA - the Storehouse
PISQACOLLCA - the Five Storehouses
▶ the Hyades

COLLCA - the Storehouse
▶ η, θ, ι, κ, λ, and υ Scorpio

CHAKANA - the Bridge
▶ the Belt of Orion

PACHAPACARIQ CHASKA - the "Venus"
of the northern suyu
▶ Altair

CHAKANA - the Bridge
▶ ε, δ, and η Canis Major

PACHAPACARIQ CHASKA - the "Venus"
of the western suyu
▶ Canopus

⊙ = Stars

◉ = Identifications in Quechua Astronomy

▨ = Dark clouds

▶ = Identifications in Western Astronomy

〜〜〜 = Approximate limits of the Milky Way (*Mayu*)

The Star-to-Star Constellations

Figure 2.8. Star-to-Star constellations as perceived by people in the region of Cuzco today. The drawing is from Urton (1981).

based on Inca concepts as described by the Spanish chroniclers. Urton found that there were two types of constellations: Star-to-Star and Dark Cloud constellations. Star-to-Star constellations link stars to form zoomorphic, geometrical, or architectural figures along or near the main path of the Milky Way (Figure 2.8). The Dark Cloud constellations are the black areas (formed of interstellar dust) that show up most distinctly, by way of contrast, in that portion of the Milky Way with the densest clustering of stars. These constellations are perceived principally as animals (Figure 2.9).[40]

Quechua people living near Cuzco thought that the Milky Way is a celestial river that is actively involved in the earth's hydrological cycle.[41] Next to the Southern Cross are the stars Alpha and Beta Centaurus, called the Eyes of the Llama. They are at the end of the Dark Cloud constellation of the Llama.[42] In the Inca period (and still today) the celestial Llama was believed to be directly

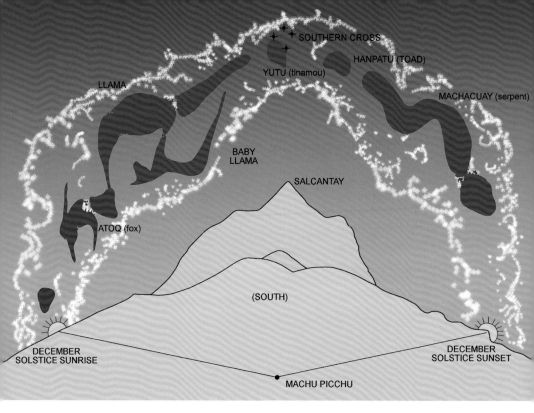

Figure 2.9. The Incas identified most of these Dark Cloud constellations in the same way as present-day villagers in the area of Cuzco. In this figure they are seen as they would appear in the rainy season. The drawing is adapted from Urton (1981).

involved with life on the earth, assisting in the circulation of its waters and in the fertility of llamas.[43] It appears in the sky before and during the rainy season, which occurs in the South American summer months.[44]

In the eastern Cuzco region the owner of llamas is believed to be Ausangate,[45] and this belief was likely held by the Incas. In the region of Salcantay livestock are thought to be under this deity's protection,[46] and this was likely the case during the Inca period. It might be added that the name *salqa* is used to denote the grazing land of livestock some 200 km west of Machu Picchu.[47] It seems reasonable to assume that there may have been a conceptual linkage between the rising of constellations associated with llamas and Salcantay, the llamas' earthly protector. Significantly, Urton noted the current-day belief among the Quechuas near Cuzco that the animals of the Dark Cloud constellations originally came from the earth and that one of the ways to enter the sky was through the summit of a mountain.[48]

Near the Llama is the Fox Dark Cloud constellation. Around the time of the December solstice the sun rises into this constellation and thus also into the Milky Way, the celestial river.[49] The fox occurs in one legend at the time of the Incas as a helper of a mountain god,[50] and is still widely perceived, including near Cuzco, as the "dog" of the mountain deities.[51] The December solstice occurs during the onset of the rainy season, when the sun rises out of the Urubamba (Vilcanota) gorge as seen from Machu Picchu and from behind Ausangate as seen from Cuzco, and it also rises into the celestial river. Ausangate is the main source of the Vilcanota River, and it is interesting that the fox not only is a helper of mountain gods but also that in some legends he helps specifically by carrying water.[52]

There are other beliefs that link Star-to-Star and Dark Cloud constellations of the Milky Way with mountains, and, assuming the beliefs were shared by the Incas, they would therefore associate them with Salcantay as seen from Machu Picchu. For example, there is a star constellation called the Serpent that is changing into the Condor (see Figure 2.8).[53] Serpents are (and were also in Inca times) associated with water in many ways in Andean beliefs (e.g., as being able to transform themselves into rivers and lightning), which are often perceived as controlled by mountain deities.[54] Condors, which soar around the highest slopes of the mountains, are widely thought in the Andes to be the representations, or manifestations, of the mountain gods; thus, it is no surprise to find that Salcantay is believed today to transform himself into one.[55]

On the opposite side of the Southern Cross are the Toad and Serpent Dark Cloud constellations (Figure 2.9). The Toad constellation rises into the sky during the rainy season.[56] Toads are commonly utilized in rituals for rain,[57] and their croaking is believed to announce the onset of rains not far from Machu Picchu.[58] We have already seen the association of serpents with water. It might be added that serpents are most active during the wet season, the time the celestial serpent is highest in the sky.[59] Thus the Southern Cross is surrounded by constellations that have to do with water, mountains, and fertility. Given the historical continuity and sharing of traditions, this was likely the case at the time of the Incas. This grouping of constellations around the summit of Salcantay at the time of the December solstice and during the onset of the rainy season would surely have been of religious and economic significance to the people of Machu Picchu.[60]

Among Quechua people living to the south of Cuzco, the Southern Cross is referred to as the Calvary Cross, a name used for a cross standing on top of a mountain.[61] These crosses are used for the protection of crops from bad weather and in some areas of the Andes are believed to represent mountain deities and to increase fertility, concepts that probably were associated in Inca thought with the Southern Cross and Salcantay.[62]

Unfortunately, there is little direct documentation of Inca beliefs about the Southern Cross.[63] The Incas, however, called a Dark Cloud constellation, a part of which is within the Southern Cross, the *yutu*. The yutu is a tinamou bird that was called by the Spanish a *perdiz* (partridge). It may be significant that the Incas sacrificed "partridges" (along with llamas) on mountaintops during the new moon and that people in the Cuzco region today consider the yutu to represent the mountain gods.[64] In addition, the eggs of the tinamou have a variety of colors resembling the rainbow.[65] Appearing together with the Southern Cross, the Tinamou constellation is also related to crop fertility, the rainy season, and thus the time that rainbows appear. Near Cuzco today the Milky Way is considered the equivalent of a nocturnal rainbow. The Tinamou constellation is in its center, together with the Southern Cross and thus above Salcantay during the onset of the rainy season.[66]

The Southern Cross appears to have been depicted in a drawing of Inca cosmology made about 1613 and within that context was interpreted as relating to fertility.[67] According to Urton it is at its highest point in the sky on the morning of the December solstice, a particularly important event associated with fertility in Inca religion.[68] Furthermore, the appearance of the Southern Cross prior to the rainy season when planting begins and its disappearance after the rains around the time of harvesting[69] suggest that its perceived association with weather and fertility by the Quechua people today was also shared by the Incas. At Machu Picchu the position of the Southern Cross in the center of the celestial river, and its alignment at its highest point in the sky with Salcantay, water, weather, and fertility in modern-day beliefs, would have made for an important combination of symbols (Figure 2.9).

In addition, Machu Picchu itself is on a ridge between rivers that have their origins from the slopes of the Salcantay massif. Salcantay not only dominates the region of Machu Picchu, but it also forms the center of a U-shaped ridge pattern, with two ridges leading north. Machu Picchu is on the tip of the eastern arm, lying along a ridge that extends due north from Salcantay via lower peaks until it meets the sacred Urubamba River (see Figures 1.10 and 2.1). A direct link exists, therefore, between the most powerful mountain deity of a vast region, astronomical phenomena, and an important Inca ritual center.

PUMASILLO

The mountain Pumasillo (6,075 m/19,931 feet) lies west of Machu Picchu and is the highest of a series of peaks forming the Sacsarayoc range (as it is called on some maps) (Figure 1.10). The name *Pumasillo* means "puma's claw," although it is unclear if this was the pre-Hispanic name for the mountain. The people of the province of La Convención, and especially in the Vilcabamba region that the range dominates, still worship the mountains of this range (and mountains closer to their villages) principally for the fertility of livestock and for crops.[70]

Although I have not found references to these mountains in the Spanish chronicles—which, in any event, mention very little about the religious beliefs of the people of this region—there can be no doubt that such worship took place at the time the Incas conquered the area in the mid-1400s. Archaeological remains such as ceremonial platforms on mountaintops in the Punkuyoc range of Vilcabamba help substantiate this likelihood (see Figure 1.10).[71]

The site of Incahuasi, on one of the summits of the Punkuyoc range, has been identified as the high mountain place visited by the Inca rebel emperor Sayri Topa when he consulted the Sun, Earth, and other deities (certainly including mountains) in 1557 about whether to accept the Spaniards' offer for him to return to Cuzco (see Figure 2.10).[72]

Figure 2.10. A perfectly preserved Inca structure at Incahuasi exists just below ritual platforms on a summit of the Punkuyoc range in the Vilcabamba region. This site lies due north of Vitcos. Views from here include Salcantay, the Pumasillo range, and other snowcapped mountains of Vilcabamba.

According to the anthropologist Stuart White, one of the higher nearby summits of the Punkuyoc range "receives in modern times enormous ritual attention from Vilcabamba residents."[73] It may be no coincidence that this mountain lies on the June solstice line for the setting sun as it extends from Machu Picchu and also supplies water to the Vilcabamba River, which in turn flows into the Vilcanota River. The mountain also lies on the legendary route of the Inca creator god, Viracocha,[74] and one of the peaks of the range, Viracochan, is named for this deity.[75]

The Pumasillo or Sacsarayoc range, with its series of peaks on the western skyline, would have served especially well for making astronomical observations from Machu Picchu (Figure 2.11). The use of mountains for such observations has been demonstrated for the Cuzco region[76] and has, indeed, been noted as common practice among native peoples throughout the Americas.[77] As seen from the Intihuatana stone at Machu Picchu, the sun sets behind the highest summit of Pumasillo (246°) at the December solstice,[78] one of the most important dates on the Inca religious calendar. The setting of the sun at the equinoxes is in line with

Figure 2.11. The Pumasillo range as viewed from Cerro San Miguel, due west from Machu Picchu. The highest summit on the left is the mountain of Pumasillo. The sun sets behind it at the December solstice. The end of the range at the right is where the sun sets at the equinoxes and also where an Inca road leads to Vitcos.

the northern end of the snowcapped peaks of this range, at which point there is an Inca trail leading to the former Inca capital of Vitcos in Vilcabamba (see Figures 1.10, 2.11, and 2.12). The Vilcabamba region was conquered by the Inca emperor Pachacuti, the likely founder of Machu Picchu, as we will see.[79]

Within Machu Picchu itself there is a building adjacent to the "Principal Temple," which was called the "Priest's House."[80] Its location and exceptional stonework indicate that it had an important religious function (see Figure 2.13). This structure is situated at the foot of the stairs leading to the Intihuatana stone, which I have interpreted as associated with mountain worship. It may be more than chance, therefore, that the doorway of the Priest's House faces out to the Pumasillo range, with its highest summit prominently in the center.

Figure 2.12. A reconstruction of what Vitcos would have looked like at the time of Inca occupation (from Lee 2000).

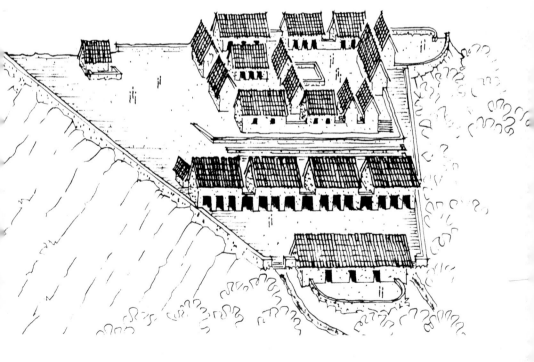

Figure 2.13. Fine Inca stonework in a wall near the Sacred Plaza at Machu Picchu.

VERONICA (WAQAYWILLKA)

The mountain range called Veronica on most maps dominates the horizon to the east of Machu Picchu (Figures 1.10 and 2.14). The highest summit (5,750 m/18,865 feet) is generally called Waqaywillka (also spelled Huacay Huilque in some accounts) by the local inhabitants. The name appears to be formed by the Quechua words *huaca*, meaning sacred place or object, and *willca* (or *vilca*), also meaning a sacred object, although apparently it also meant the sun in ancient times.[81] The Incas frequently applied the term *uaca bilca* (*waqa willka*) to local deities, especially mountains.[82]

It is also possible that the name derives from *willki*, meaning spirit of a "peak," and *waqay*, meaning "to cry."[83] According to a local ritual specialist, Luciano Carbajal, the tears refer to the many streams that flow from the mountain and to their association with rain, which is controlled by Veronica, as well as Salcantay (along with other major mountains of the region).[84] Veronica and Salcantay communicate with each other using voices of thunder, which obviously is associated with rain.

Figure 2.14. The Veronica range dominates the eastern skyline as seen from Cerro San Miguel. Machu Picchu is in the lower center of the picture, and the highest summit of Veronica is the snowcapped peak in the center, lying due east. The other main summit of the range is to the left and is visible from the Intihuatana.

Figure 2.15. Tourists ascend steps at Machu Picchu with Veronica in the background.

One of Veronica's principal summits is visible from Machu Picchu (e.g., from the Intihuatana stone [see Figure 2.15]), and the highest summit is visible from prominences near Machu Picchu, such as Huayna Picchu, Machu Picchu Mountain, and Cerro San Miguel (see Figure 1.10). At the equinoxes the sun rises behind the highest summit. This combination of a snowcapped sacred mountain and the rising of the sun at the equinoxes would have added to the reverence paid to this mountain. It might also explain the use of the word *willka*, with its semantic connotations of "sacred" and "sun." Still today stars, including the sun, are believed to acquire a greater amount of power when they become associated with a sacred mountain.[85]

This mountain is also referred to as "Eterno Abuelo" (Eternal Grandfather or Ancestor) and, as a variation, "Padre Eterno" (Eternal Father).[86] These names, and ones with a similar meaning, are also applied to other sacred mountains.[87] They serve as terms of respect for the mountains, which are viewed in many areas as protectors (like fathers) and may also have been seen by earlier inhabitants as their places of origin.[88] Some people attribute these names specifically to the slightly lower summit of the Veronica range visible from the Intihuatana stone at Machu Picchu.

As one would expect, Veronica is still highly revered by people in the region. It is worshipped for the fertility of crops, livestock, and good health.[89] Like other major mountains, it can provide *illas*, which are stones often shaped like livestock and thought to be gifts of the mountain deities for increasing the size of herds.[90]

Dominating as it does an important road linking the highlands with the tropical lowlands, Veronica receives offerings from travelers and businessmen for the success of their journeys. During the Inca period roads passed below the mountain to the south along the Urubamba River and to the north via a high pass. This latter route became the principal road used to reach Vilcabamba from Cuzco after the Spanish conquest (Figure 1.10).

Above the Inca quarry to the south of the Urubamba River near Ollantaytambo there are Inca structures (artificial platforms, one with a doorway that frames Veronica) at elevations of 3,900 m/12,795 feet and 4,450 m/14,560 feet built on prominences that provide excellent views toward Veronica (Figure 2.16).[91] On the opposite side of the river on the slopes of Veronica at ca. 4,050 m/13,287 feet is another artificial platform with a dominating view of the mountain.[92] These types of structures were primarily for ceremonial use, as will be noted below, and thus provide archaeological evidence supporting Veronica's religious importance during the Inca period.

Figure 2.16. The town of Ollantaytambo with the mountain Veronica (Waqaywillka) looming above.

MOUNTAIN WORSHIP IN THE ANDES

There are some common elements of mountain worship in the Andes, especially relating to the large snowcapped peaks, which we have seen can apply to the mountains in the region of Machu Picchu. Based on the historical and ethnographic evidence, one of the most important of these elements is the belief that the high mountains control weather and thus the fertility of crops and animals. This belief is based on ecological reality, since meteorological phenomena (rain, snow, hail, clouds, lightning, thunder, etc.) often originate in the mountains.[93] Other common elements should be examined to help us better understand the role mountain worship could have had in the region.

A social cohesion, in some cases even an ethnic identity, could have revolved around worship of these sacred mountains, just as has been noted for many areas of the Andes, for example, Ayacucho,[94] the region north of Lake Titicaca,[95] central Bolivia,[96] Huancavelica,[97] and in the region of Cuzco.[98] This was also clearly the case in prehispanic times.[99]

Social cohesion would have brought with it political ramifications. For example, mountains may have been perceived as protectors and war gods of the peoples who lived near them and worshipped them.[100] To consolidate their rule, the Incas may have attempted to appropriate this association with the mountains by constructing special places of worship such as Machu Picchu.[101]

Throughout the Andes, mountain deities were also believed to be the owners of wild animals.[102] This was the case in the Cuzco region as well.[103] Hunting of wild animals was thus linked to the mountains.[104] In the rugged area of Machu Picchu, which had a large number of wild animals (pumas, bears, poisonous snakes, birds, and so forth), their presence would have provided an additional reason for mountain worship. (As noted above, the Quechua word for "wild" is *salqa* and forms the root of the name Salcantay.) It might be added that Topa Inca, who took the place of his father Pachacuti (probable builder of Machu Picchu, as we will see) while he still lived, was said to have been a keen hunter.[105]

I have referred briefly to the important role that mountain deities played with regard to domesticated animals. Llamas and alpacas played a vital role in the economy of the Incas, and throughout the Andes mountain deities are perceived as their owners and as responsible for their fertility.[106] The same beliefs are also held in the Cuzco region.[107] As we have seen, Ausangate is perceived as the owner of these animals in the region of Cuzco.[108] Llamas were used to transport goods in the region of Machu Picchu, but they also grazed close to the mountains, providing yet another reason for the importance of mountain worship. Because of their association with pack animals and with prosperity in general, mountain deities were invoked for success in trade,[109] just as they are today.[110]

The Spanish priest Bernabé Cobo noted that the Vilcabamba region was rich in mineral wealth, which the Incas exploited.[111] The only mines near Machu Picchu of which I am aware that may have been originally worked by the Incas are at the headwaters of the Aobamba River and the Pampa Qhawana River, both of which are at the foot of Salcantay.[112] It remains to be seen, therefore, whether mining played a role in Machu Picchu's importance. It might be added, however, that mining invariably involved worship of mountain gods, who were believed to be the owners of the minerals.[113] Thus, even if mining was associated with Machu Picchu, it would not affect the interpretation presented here.

As we have seen in the case of Salcantay, ritual specialists are widely believed to receive their power from the sacred mountains. Only the most experienced and knowledgeable of these specialists could deal directly with the highest and most powerful mountains.[114] Such specialists invoke the mountain gods to cure illnesses, foretell the future, find lost objects, help people obtain prosperity and success in business, and perform rituals on behalf of the community for the fertility of crops and animals (Figure 2.17).

Figure 2.17. A ritual specialist (paqo) burns offerings to the mountain gods (apus) near Cuzco.

Figure 2.18. The Urubamba River circles Machu Picchu and Huayna Picchu in this view from the summit of Machu Picchu Mountain looking north. The lower peaks of the Veronica massif form the skyline.

We know that the Inca emperor considered ritual specialists who served the mountain deities to be especially privileged, and he personally supported these men.[115] Machu Picchu's unique setting amidst the most powerful mountains of the region would have made it an ideal place not only for worship of the mountains but also for receiving their powers and perhaps serving as a center for initiations to them, much as ritual places in the mountains are utilized today.

Mountains, therefore, were worshipped for many reasons, including the fertility of domesticated camelids and crops, trade, curing of illnesses, weather control, protection from enemies, control of wild animals, and empowerment of ritual specialists. But worship was not limited to great mountains such as Salcantay, Pumasillo, and Veronica; lesser mountains near Machu Picchu would also have played important roles.

HUAYNA PICCHU

We have already seen Machu Picchu's direct physical link with Salcantay. The sacred Urubamba River nearly encircles the promontory where the site is located, likely adding to the sacredness of the mountain that dominates it, Huayna Picchu (Figure 2.18). This mountain, which serves as the backdrop to the classic view of Machu Picchu, marks the end of the ridge before it plunges to the Urubamba River below. It was for this reason that the steep gorge thus formed became known as the "Gateway of Salcantay."[116]

Huayna Picchu is framed as one enters through the main Inca gateway into Machu Picchu (Figure 2.19). It overlooks the site (being 207 m/679 feet higher) and commands a magnificent view: the main peaks of the Veronica range to the east, the snowcapped peaks of the Pumasillo range to the west, and the summit of Salcantay to the south (Figure 2.20).

The archaeological remains, such as carvings of a ceremonial nature in boulders, on and near the summit of Huayna Picchu[117] help to substantiate that it was considered sacred by the Incas, as does the Temple of the Moon down on its western slope, which is linked to the summit by an impressive trail cut through a cliff face. Hills that dominate communities in the Cuzco and Vilcabamba regions, whether in Inca or modern times, are invariably viewed as being local protector deities and usually are responsible, at least in part, for the fertility of crops and livestock.[118] We would expect that Huayna Picchu played a similar role with regard to Machu Picchu.

Figure 2.19. The main gateway at Machu Picchu frames Huayna Picchu.

Figure 2.20. Looking south from the summit of Huayna Picchu, the tip of Salcantay (marked by an arrow) is behind the central peak of the skyline. In the lower part of the photo is a V-shaped carving in a stone, and a similar one is found near the Intihuatana below.

MACHU PICCHU MOUNTAIN

Overlooking Machu Picchu to the south lies the mountain for which it was named (Figure 2.21). It is some 500 m/1,640 feet higher than the ruins, and a very well-made stairway leads from Machu Picchu to its summit. On top is a series of interconnected artificial platforms that have been heavily damaged by treasure hunters. Although Bingham called this summit complex a "signal station," it clearly was more than that.[119]

As in the case of Huayna Picchu, Machu Picchu Mountain would probably have been perceived as a local protector deity. Artificial platforms similar to those on its summit have been found on mountain summits near Cuzco, such as on Cerro Pinta and Pachatusan, and even exist at ca. 6,700 m (21,981 feet) in the southern Andes.[120] These had a religious function, as is clear from the Inca ritual offerings found buried in them (not for nothing have the platforms on Machu Picchu Mountain been extensively dug into by treasure hunters), the extensive system of structures and roads leading to and up the mountains (hardly necessary for only making signals), the sacredness of the mountains themselves, and

Figure 2.21. Machu Picchu Mountain dominates the background in this view from the hilltop of the Intihuatana. The Sacred Plaza is in the lower part of the picture along with the Principal Temple. To its left is the Temple of Three Windows.

the negligible role that signal stations could have played on the higher peaks in a system of communications.[121] This does not mean that the platforms could not have served as places from which to send signals in some cases, but this purpose would have been of secondary importance compared to the religious-political-economic factors involved in worship of the mountains themselves.

There is another reason for Machu Picchu Mountain's importance. Bingham noted that there were several springs on the side of this mountain that were utilized by people at Machu Picchu to supply water.[122] Sources of water were (and still are) in themselves sacred and made up a substantial number of the sacred places surrounding Cuzco, as noted by Cobo in the mid-1600s.[123] But of particular interest is a common belief in the Cuzco region that water originating lower down on the slopes of a mountain originates inside the mountain itself.[124] West of Cuzco springs are even seen as the entrances used by the mountain gods.[125]

As I noted with regard to the ruins of Machu Picchu, they (and thus Machu Picchu Mountain) do not exist in isolation but rather are on a ridge that extends down from Salcantay. Given the nature of Inca beliefs, it is not unlikely that the water that led through Machu Picchu was thought to take on part of the sacred character of Salcantay. These waters would in turn have been used in the ritual fountains at the site and may have been utilized to some degree for irrigation. The mountains, subterranean waters, irrigation systems, and river flow would thus have been united in a sacred hydraulic chain.[126]

When I began this discussion of the sacred geography of the Machu Picchu region, I noted that one river in particular played an important role at the site, and we should now examine why this was so.

THE URUBAMBA (VILCANOTA) RIVER

A legend of the Quechua people living near Cuzco links the daily rebirth of the sun with its passage beneath the Vilcanota River, whose waters it drinks to regain its brightness.[127] (The name of the river changes from Vilcanota to Urubamba before it reaches Machu Picchu.) The Vilcanota River runs southeast to northwest (until beyond Machu Picchu) (Figure 2.4), and it is considered the terrestrial reflection of the daytime path of the sun during the period surrounding the December solstice.[128] Between the months of November and February the axis of the Milky Way runs southeast to northwest, with one end being near the position of the rising sun at the December solstice, and the sun rises at this time into the Milky Way.[129]

According to current-day beliefs the sun follows the course of the Vilcanota River underground during the night to rise again the next day in the east.[130] The rainy period intensifies after the December solstice, when the flow of the rivers increases and the growing season begins. The legend does not specifically refer to the region farther downriver to Machu Picchu, nor is there historical documentation of the same beliefs being held by the Incas, but there is evidence that this was the case, as we will see.

Based on the above, it would seem that it was not by chance that the name *Vilcanota* meant "house of the sun" or "house where the sun was born" in the language of the Aymara people, presumably because the river (and the mountain range of the same name at its source) flows along the sun's path as seen from Cuzco.[131] The Vilcanota River is also equated today with the celestial river, the Milky Way,[132] and probably was during the Inca period as well.

The Vilcanota River has its principal sources of origin in the snows of Ausangate and in the snows of mountains (associated in contemporary beliefs with Ausangate) located above the Pass of La Raya, southeast of Cuzco (see Figures 2.4 and 2.22). All rivers that have their sources in Ausangate are seen today to partake of its powers and sacred character.[133] In addition, the snows of other sacred mountains, including Veronica and Salcantay, also feed this river. It is widely believed that such water is a fertilizing agent of the mountain gods.[134]

The river itself is viewed as an important deity among people in the Cuzco region today.[135] Its sacred character at the time of the Incas is demonstrated by important ruins at its source,[136] which were associated with the temple of Vilcanota (located at the Pass of La Raya), noted as one of the most important in the Inca Empire (Figure 2.22).[137] This is also supported by our knowledge of the religious significance of rivers in Inca thought and, of course, by the numerous Inca sites of importance, including Pisac and Ollantaytambo, found along the Vilcanota/Urubamba River's course until passing by Machu Picchu. (6)

After completing his acts of creation at Lake Titicaca, the Inca deity Viracocha is believed to have followed a route in his journey from the lake to the ocean that followed a SE–NW line (i.e., paralleling the general course of the Vilcanota River) until well beyond Machu Picchu.[138] Urton believes that Viracocha can be equated in Inca thought with the Vilcanota River and the Milky Way.[139] Viracocha was certainly closely associated with water cults and mountains,[140] and important temples devoted to him, such as at Rajchi and Viracochan (southeast of Cuzco), were located along the Vilcanota River.[141] (Indeed, the river sets off the mountain of Viracochan by making a loop around it, much as it does at Machu Picchu.) This may be one reason that two statues of Viracocha were reportedly kept at Amaybamba,[142] a place along the river of the same name not far from Machu

Figure 2.22. The pass of La Raya, location of the Temple of Vilcanota, origin of the Vilcanota (Urubamba) River and final destination of an annual pilgrimage made by the Incas.

Picchu, which flowed into the Vilcanota River (see Figure 1.10). A third statue was kept in the same area near the bridge above Chaullay that crossed the river and led to Vilcabamba.[143] It does not seem mere coincidence that above the region in which the statues were located is another mountain named Viracochan (Figure 1.10).[144] (7)

What we have, then, is a river with a conceptual tie with the passage, and even birth, of the sun. The river's origin is also directly linked to Ausangate, one of the two major mountain deities of the entire Cuzco region. The river makes a virtual loop around Machu Picchu and Huayna Picchu, which are themselves at the end of an arm of Salcantay, the other principal mountain deity (Figure 1.10). The river passage as a whole roughly follows the path of the sun, which rises during the December solstice from behind Ausangate (only to set, as seen from Machu Picchu, behind another of the major snow peaks—and provider of water—Pumasillo). It also is in accord with the legendary journey of the Inca creator deity, Viracocha.

When the river winds around Machu Picchu, the outer part of the loop is on its north side, while Salcantay lies due south. In addition, the Aobamba and Cusichaka rivers, which set off the Machu Picchu sanctuary sites north and south of the famous Inca Trail and flow into the Urubamba River, both have their principal origins from the snows of Salcantay. The Southern Cross, at the center of the Milky Way (the celestial water source in Inca thought), appears above Salcantay when it reaches its highest point in the sky. The people at Machu Picchu would have been well aware of the sun rising from behind Ausangate (even though the mountain was not visible from Machu Picchu) and setting behind Pumasillo at the December solstice.

As we have seen, the Incas had an intense concern with the sun's passage, with sacred mountains, and with the orientation of water flow.[145] Clearly, the unique combination of these elements at Machu Picchu would have led to its being considered an especially powerful sacred center.

Chapter Three

Architecture and Sacred Landscape

Since there are no historical records or oral traditions that deal directly with architecture at Machu Picchu, any interpretation must be based on comparisons with Inca structures elsewhere, on our knowledge of Inca beliefs, on ethnographic data, and on logical deductions formed from examinations of the architecture's features within the natural settings. It would seem obvious that, if the reasons for Machu Picchu's location and primary functions were related to sacred landscape in conjunction with celestial orientations and a hydrological cycle, we can expect that such factors would be reflected in some of the prominent architectural features at the site (Figure 3.1).

Although speculative, the presentation of hypotheses to explain some structures should assist in provoking a closer examination of their functions and placing them within the broader context of which they are a part. This may be premature given the lack of material available on Machu Picchu, but avoiding the issue does not serve science and instead leaves a vacuum that leads to many highly improbable interpretations, such as can be heard daily by visitors to the site. Alternative explanations to those I present can be found in some of the principal publications referred to in the text, beginning with Hiram Bingham's (1979) main work, and they will not be dealt with in detail here.

Figure 3.1a: The layout of Machu Picchu can best be seen looking south from Huanacauri.

To Inca Bridge

Inca Trail

scale

0   50 m.

Figure 3.1b. A plan of Machu Picchu. (Plan courtesy of Kenneth Wright 2000).

To Wayna
Picchu, Temple
of the Moon

1 Terrace Caretaker's Houses
  (main entrance)
2 Agricultural Sector
3 Dry Moat
4 Ritual Baths
5 Principal Bath
6 Temple of the Sun (Torreón)
7 "Palace of the Princess"
8 "Fountain Caretaker's Houes"
9 Royal Sector
10 Watchman's Hut
11 Funerary Rock
12 Quarry
13 Temple of the Three Windows
14 Principal Temple
15 "Sacristy"
16 Intihuatana
17 Sacred Rock
18 Common District
19 Mortar Building
20 "Prison Group" or "Condor
   Temple"
21 Intimachay

TEMPLES ON THE SACRED PLAZA

Many visitors to Machu Picchu begin their tour by obtaining an overview of the site from a location near what has come to be called the Watchman's House (also Guardhouse) (Figures 3.2 and 3.3). It is adjacent to the so-called Terrace of the Ceremonial Rock, around which can be seen a number of river stones—probably used during Inca times in rituals to invoke water and fertility (Figure 3.4). Inca pilgrims would have passed by the same location on their way to enter the site through the main gateway (Figure 3.5). After passing through the gateway, the trail leads to some of the most impressive structures at Machu Picchu, forming part of what Bingham called the Sacred Plaza (Figure 3.6).[146]

Bordering the plaza on its north side is the Principal Temple, which is open to the south and contains a large, carved stone altar (Figure 3.7). Bingham excavated the floor of this structure, but he did not find any artifacts of note. He was surprised, however, to discover a layer of white sand. Although sand was occasionally utilized in other Inca structures,[147] the use of white sand in this setting calls to mind the sand found in the plazas of Haucaypata and Cusipata in Cuzco.[148] Here the sand was brought from the Pacific coast (presumably done at the order of the emperor Pachacuti when he had Cuzco rebuilt) and said to be offered in reverence to the creator deity Ticsi Viracocha.[149] He was called this name when

Figure 3.2. Overview of Machu Picchu from near the Watchman's House.

Figure 3.3. The Watchman's House and llama.

he was associated with the ocean,[150] and, as we have seen, three idols of Viracocha were located not far below Machu Picchu. The presence of sand in the plaza suggests that the ocean (mother of all waters) was seen as being ritually placed in the religious center of Cuzco.[151] Keeping in mind information presented above and that Machu Picchu was a center likely built by Pachacuti, it would seem reasonable to assume that this was the case at the Principal Temple as well.

Whereas the ocean is thought of as the origin of all waters, the mountains are perceived as controllers of the waters.[152] For this reason seawater and seashells are often used in rituals for rain carried out on mountain summits in the Andes.[153] We could, therefore, see the use of sand in the floor of the Principal Temple, open in the direction of Machu Picchu Mountain and Salcantay (and associated celestial phenomena), as playing a role in a mountain/water cult. On the east side of the Sacred Plaza is a beautifully built structure that Bingham named the Temple of the Three Windows (Figure 3.8). He noted the uniqueness of such large windows in an Inca building and the obvious ceremonial nature of the structure.[154] The windows look out toward the mountains and Urubamba River to the east, while the structure is open to the west with a clear view to the Pumasillo range (Figure 3.9).

Figure 3.4. River rocks are found scattered around the "ceremonial stone" near the Watchman's House.

Excavations beneath the Temple of the Three Windows and elsewhere near the Sacred Plaza unearthed shards of 66 vessels. Of these vessels, 56 were for holding liquids (see Figure 3.10).[155] It could be argued that such a percentage would hold for pottery found at any ceremonial site whatever its purpose. The discovery, however, of vessels for holding liquids so near the area of sand at the center of a site that likely was associated with water/weather ceremonies would suggest that the vessels were used in such rites. The many shards found below the windows indicate that the vessels may have been ritually broken, a practice that took place in pre-Inca times and is still common in the Andes today.[156] (Most of the intact vessels collected by Bingham came from burials, some of which were accessible under boulders and likely received offerings during the Inca period; see Figure 3.11.) This hypothesis is further strengthened when we place these finds and ceremonial structures within the context of Machu Picchu's sacred geographical setting and in view of my interpretation of the Intihuatana stone (see below), which is on a hill overlooking the Sacred Plaza and connected to it by the most carefully constructed stairway at Machu Picchu. (8)

SACRED STONES

Some of the stones at Machu Picchu have been carved or set off in such a way that clearly indicates they were either worshipped in themselves or used as places of worship. It will not be possible to examine the majority of such stones here, but a few comments should be made as to how they fit into an interpretation of Machu Picchu in terms of sacred geography. Before examining some of the stones at Machu Picchu, we should take a look at beliefs held about stones in traditional Andean religion.

In this brief overview I am primarily concerned with stones or boulders that are not moveable, although this does not mean they do not share characteristics with ones that have been set up artificially. Examining the literature, we find that large stones are often believed to house spirits, and in some cases these spirits are those of ancestors.[157] When found next to fields or villages, they are frequently perceived as protector spirits and as capable of increasing productivity. This is the case near Cuzco today,[158] and similar beliefs were held in prehispanic times over a large area of Peru.[159]

Figure 3.5. The main gateway at Machu Picchu.

Figure 3.6. The Sacred Plaza, in the lower left center of the picture, was aptly named by Bingham because of the religious nature of the structures surrounding it. The Principal Temple is visible with finely carved steps leading up from it to the Intihuatana stone (behind the structure in the upper left center). Huayna Picchu is the mountain in the background on the right.

Stones were also noted throughout the Andes as representing mountain gods.[160] Near Cuzco stones were worshipped on mountains such as Huanacauri,[161] and we know that a stone shaped like this mountain was worshipped outside of Cuzco.[162] Boulders at villages are still worshipped because of their association with major mountains of the area, such as Ausangate.[163] Given the above, it is easy to understand why Bernabé Cobo, writing in the mid-1600s, listed stones as making up 29 percent of the sacred objects around Cuzco.[164]

Turning now specifically to stones at Machu Picchu, we first have to establish what evidence can be used to determine the possible function of a stone in terms of sacred geography. (9) Since there is no direct historical evidence and the reasons that boulders were worshipped were not always the same, we have to look at each stone relative to its location within the site and see if its shape, how it was viewed (following the approach to it constructed by the Incas), and nearby items would help in establishing its function (e.g., if sacred geographical features were replicated). I am aware of only a few cases where these factors appear to come together, but these are significant ones.

THE INTIHUATANA

The Intihuatana stone is the centerpiece of a prominent ritual site at the ruins. It was named Intihuatana by Bingham because of its resemblance to similar carved stones near Cuzco that had been previously called by this term, which means roughly "the place to which the sun was tied."[165] According to John Rowe this name does not appear in the literature until 1856, where is was applied to a "huge block" above the Inca site at Ollantaytambo.[166]

Most discussions of the Intihuatana have interpreted it as a sundial, but doubts about this were expressed as long ago as 1910.[167] Recent studies by astronomers have been unable to see how the Intihuatana might have served such a function.[168] Even if the angles carved on the stone should prove to have had some role in astronomical observations,[169] that still would not rule out its having played a role in mountain worship, as we will see below.

It is significant that, viewed from the Intihuatana at Machu Picchu, sacred mountains are in alignment with the cardinal directions. The Veronica range lies to the east, and the sun rises behind its highest summit at the equinoxes (cf. Figures 1.10, 2.14, 3.12, and 3.13). Huayna Picchu is due north (Figure 3.14). A line of snowcapped peaks of the Pumasillo range is to the west, the sun setting behind the highest summit (246°) at the December solstice and the equinox line crossing

Figure 3.7. This structure was named the Principal Temple by Hiram Bingham. Sand was found to cover the floor of the temple.

Figure 3.8. The beautifully carved windows that gave rise to the name Temple of the Three Windows. It borders the eastern side of the Sacred Plaza.

its northern end (Figures 1.10, 2.11, and 3.15). The massif of Salcantay lies to the south, its highest summit being at an azimuth of precisely 180°. Salcantay is not visible from the Intihuatana, but it is visible from the summits of Huayna Picchu and Machu Picchu peak (see Figure 2.20). The Intihuatana was, therefore, at a central point from which sacred mountains were in alignment with the cardinal directions and where significant celestial activity took place (see appendix).

The Intihuatana is also well situated for other astronomical observations. The setting sun at the equinoxes occurs behind the highest summit of Cerro San Miguel (272°) (Figures 3.15 and 3.16). The sun can be seen to rise from behind Cerro San Gabriel at the June solstice at 61° (Figure 3.13)[170] and to set behind the San Miguel ridge at 297°. (As a result of the higher elevation on the horizon of the nearest peaks, there is a slight deviation from those azimuths taken when the sunrises and sunsets are viewed across an open, horizontal plane.) The sun at the December solstice rises out of the Urubamba River valley at 112° (Figure 3.13). The Southern Cross would have been seen to move around Machu Picchu

Mountain.[171] Thus the location of the Intihuatana on a high point of a ridge gave it an exceptional place from which to make astronomical observations in conjunction with sacred geographical features, helping make Machu Picchu a center of special supernatural power.

The shape of the Intihuatana resembles that of a mountain. This is particularly striking when one juxtaposes it with Huayna Picchu. The shadows cast on the Intihuatana also are replicated by those on Huayna Picchu (Figure 3.14). Even the base of the vertical stone appears to imitate the shape of the lower part of Huayna Picchu. This alignment occurs when one enters the summit compound by its main entrance and ascends the left-hand steps to the Intihuatana and looks toward it. There is only one other set of steps that lead to the Intihuatana from the temple area below. These are wider and just to the right of the first set; perhaps they were meant to be used by people not taking part in the worship performed at the boulder to the left. Carved into the boulder next to where the steps end is a V-shaped depression "pointing" south, which, given its location, was likely used as a place for offerings.

A similar rock carving is found on the summit of Huayna Picchu. It "points" due south in the direction of the Intihuatana and Salcantay (Figure 2.20). The placement of one set of steps and the V-shaped depression would appear intentional, establishing a place for someone to view the Intihuatana in alignment with Huayna Picchu. This would indicate that the Intihuatana was carved to replicate the mountain.

Interestingly, if a person stands on the opposite side of the Intihuatana and looks south, its shape seems to replicate that of Machu Picchu Mountain and its northern slope (Figure 3.17). If this was intentional on the part of the Incas, the Intihuatana would be simultaneously duplicating the shapes of the two sacred mountains closest to Machu Picchu. This would provide an unusual example in worked stone of the kind of reflexivity that has been noted for some Inca sites and structures located elsewhere, including near Machu Picchu, as we will see.

As far as the Intihuatana having been used as a kind of solar observatory, it quite possibly was, but in a different way from that postulated by the sundial theory. Traditional peoples in the Cuzco region still use the movements of shadows across the mountains to tell time, and in the past they observed shadows on vertical stones for the same purpose.[172] Thus observations could have been made of the sun's movements across the Intihuatana (which replicated a sacred mountain) while those movements were also being made on the mountain itself (i.e., Huayna Picchu). This would be different from simply observing the shadow cast on a flat surface by the column of a sundial in order to tell time and would be a more powerful melding of natural symbols as well.

Figure 3.9. A view to the west from in front of the Temple of the Three Windows. The arrow points to the summit of Pumasillo. The Principal Temple is on the right.

The evidence points to Rowe's having been correct when he stated that the Intihuatana may have symbolized the "place spirit" of the mountain on which it stands.[173] I mentioned earlier that the Incas worshipped a stone having the shape of the sacred mountain Huanacauri, and this is just one of several examples of the Incas having undertaken the kind of replication noted here (see Guchte 1990). (10) Additional support for this hypothesis comes from a drawing done in 1613 of sacred objects and idols. In it the Inca Topa is portrayed as questioning some idols that have the shape of the Intihuatana (Figure 3.18).[174] He is asking which one was responsible for causing bad weather, a role often attributed to mountain deities. Certainly if Machu Picchu was built with a primary factor being its situation relative to sacred geographical features, then it would be logical for one of its outstanding landmarks, a prominent carved stone, to serve as the symbolic representation of a sacred mountain.

Figure 3.10. The aribalo (arybalo) was mainly used to hold liquids, and it was common among the pottery found by Bingham at Machu Picchu. Its form is distinctive to the Incas. (This example from the Inca site on Mount Llullaillaco was recovered with its original rope in place.)

Figure 3.11. Skulls of ancestors were still being worshipped along the Inca Trail in Huayllabamba during the 1980s.

THE SACRED ROCK

There is another boulder that some investigators believe replicates the shape of a mountain,[175] a particularly prominent boulder found at the north end of the site. It has come to be called the Sacred Rock by some authors, although there are, of course, many other sacred rocks at Machu Picchu. This one has been singled out because of its large size, its demarcation by a stone platform on one side of an open square, its similarity in shape to the contours of one of the mountains in the background, and its location between two stone buildings with the third side open.

The main entry to the Sacred Rock complex via this open third side does seem to indicate that the stone was meant to be viewed with the mountains in the background. An exact fit with any one of these mountains is difficult, however, to discern, the mountain Yanantin coming closest (Figure 3.19).

The anthropologist Robert Randall noted that if a person turned to look out the one open side of the Sacred Rock complex, he or she would be facing

Figure 3.12. Sunrise as seen from Machu Picchu.

Pumasillo, which does indeed replicate the shape of the Sacred Rock.[176] We may also have another example of reflexivity involving sacred mountains on opposite sides of a carved boulder, as noted above. Although it is not firmly established whether the Sacred Rock was worshipped as representing a mountain, given the above and my interpretation of Machu Picchu as a whole, this explanation seems reasonable.

THE SUN TEMPLE (TORREÓN)

Additional stones clearly meant for ritual use are the large stones into which platforms or altars have been carved. One of the best-known examples of this is a carved boulder found inside the structure named the Semicircular Temple by Bingham and now commonly called the Temple of the Sun or the Torreón

Figure 3.13. Looking east from the Intihuatana, which is in the foreground. The left arrow marks the rising point of the sun at the June solstice, the center one the rising point of the sun at the equinoxes, and the right one the rising point of the sun at the December solstice (above the Urubamba River gorge).

Figure 3.14. The Intihuatana stone appears to replicate the shape of, and the play of shadows on, Huayna Picchu in the background. Even the base of the stone appears to be carved to represent in an abstract manner the shape of the mountain.

Figure 3.15. A view to the west from the Intihuatana. The arrow on the left points to the summit of Pumasillo behind which the sun sets at the December solstice. The arrow on the right indicates the point (on the summit of Cerro San Miguel) where the sun sets at the equinoxes.

(see Figures 3.20 and 3.21).[177] The walls built around the carved boulder contain some of the finest Inca stonework known, and the rare, elliptical form of the structure recalls that of the Temple of the Sun (Coricancha) in Cuzco (Figure 3.22).

The top of the boulder inside the Temple of the Sun apparently was utilized as an altar. By use of a carving in its surface, it may also have served as an aid in making observations of the June solstice (Figure 3.23).[178] Since the position where the Pleiades rise is close to that of the sun at the June solstice,[179] a window orientated to one included the other. The Pleiades were (and still are) closely associated with crop fertility and the forecasting of weather.[180] (11) The Pleiades are due north when they reach their highest point in the sky, and thus they will also be above Huayna Picchu. This juxtaposition thereby presents a parallel to the Southern Cross and Salcantay to the south.

When the sun shines through the window onto the carving of the rock at the June solstice, it also appears from behind the top of the peak called, by some locals, San Gabriel.[181] Although it is one of the lower mountains of the Veronica

Figure 3.17. A view south to the Intihuatana with Machu Picchu Mountain in the background. Here, too, it appears to replicate the shape of, and the play of shadows on, a mountain in the background. Just behind the Intihuatana are two sets of steps that worshippers used to reach the sacred stone.

Figure 3.18. An Inca is depicted worshipping at a carved stone that resembles the Intihuatana at Machu Picchu (from Guaman Poma 1980 [1613]).

Figure 3.19. Called by some the Sacred Rock, this boulder was especially demarcated by a stone wall at its base. It may have been set off in order to replicate the shape of the mountain Yanantin (directly behind it) in the background (San Gabriel is on the right). The boulder is more similar, however, to Pumasillo, visible in the opposite direction, which is the only open side of the complex.

range, it is nonetheless notable as seen from Machu Picchu. It would seem that in this case there is a direct link between astronomical observations and mountains, where the celestial body (and the place from which it was observed—in this case a carved boulder) gains in importance because of its association with a prominent peak on the horizon. We have already seen the importance of the Veronica range in beliefs relating to weather and fertility.

The large boulder inside the Temple of the Sun also forms the top of a cave, and this would probably have added to the building's sacredness (Figure 3.24). The cave contains beautifully carved stones and niches, which led Bingham to believe it was used as a royal mausoleum (see Figure 3.25).[182] From the cave's entrance one can look out toward San Gabriel and surrounding mountains. At the entrance is a boulder carved in a stepped pattern that some authors believe was commonly used to symbolize a mountain,[183] an interpretation that would also be in accord with that of the Temple of the Sun above. There is other evidence pertaining to beliefs about caves in Inca thought to support the hypothesis that the cave was associated with mountain worship, which I will examine below.

TEMPLE OF THE MOON

The Temple of the Moon is actually a cave situated some 390 m/1,280 feet below the summit of Huayna Picchu on its steep northern side. It contains some very fine Inca stonework (Figure 3.26). Apparently the cave was given its name by people in modern times who observed that during the night of a full moon the cave's interior became illuminated.[184] It is probably of greater importance that it looks out at the equinox setting point of the sun on the ridge of Cerro San Miguel, which coincides with the place on the horizon where the sun sets on the June solstice as seen from the Intihuatana.

Since not all caves received such special treatment, we should examine what elements could have played a role in the high status bestowed on this one. It is possible that water, fairly scarce in this area, came out of a spring near the cave or even from inside it.[185] The location of the cave high on the sacred mountain of Huayna Picchu could also have been a factor.

When we examine beliefs about caves in the Andes, there are shared features that could help explain the special attention paid to this one. Historical sources note that caves were often perceived as the entrances into the mountains from which the first ancestors came, and frequently bodies of dead ancestors were kept in caves. Such beliefs and practices were in many cases linked to the concept that people came out from the mountains through caves and that the souls themselves return to reside there.

Caves are seen as the entrances into the mountains where the mountain gods reside in many parts of Peru.[186] This belief was noted in the Inca period,[187] and it still exists in the area of Cuzco today.[188] Similar beliefs are held as far afield as Bolivia and Chile.[189] Caves could also be seen as entrances into the mountains that animals, believed to belong to the mountain gods, could use as well. In addition, caves were places for leaving offerings to the mountain deities.[190]

Archaeologists have made recent discoveries below the Temple of the Moon that appear to support the interpretation that it was related to mountain worship. They found a structure that had two small holes in two niches. The only thing visible when looking through the holes was a prominent mountain across the river called Yanantin.[191] The archaeologists believe that the holes were made as part of practices done in worship of this sacred mountain. Yanantin is the same mountain that may have been replicated by the Sacred Rock.

Taken as a whole, the evidence points to the Temple of the Moon having become important, at least in part, as a result of its association with mountain worship. Perhaps its opening out, albeit only in a general way, toward the setting sun at the equinoxes (which in turn occur at the same place where the June solstice sets as seen from the Intihuatana) added to its sacredness.

Figure 3.20. View to the Sun Temple (Torreón) with the Intihuatana hill behind.

Figure 3.21. The Sun Temple is one of the best-constructed structures at Machu Picchu. The boulder inside it may have been carved partly to serve as an altar and also to observe the rise of the sun and the Pleiades at the [...] solstice through a window orientated in that direction.

Figure 3.22. The elliptical wall of the Temple of the Sun (Coricancha) in Cuzco is one of the most astonishing examples of Inca stonework. The Dominican Church was constructed over the temple's remains.

INTIMACHAY AND THE CONDOR STONE

Intimachay is a small cave that also has some fine Inca stonework indicating that it was of special significance to the Incas. It is located on the eastern side of Machu Picchu, just below what has been named the "Industrial Quarter" on some plans of the site. A convincing case has been made that it was built primarily as a place to observe the December solstice sunrise.[192] As seen from Machu Picchu, on the December solstice the sun does not rise behind any noteworthy feature of the horizon. Below the immediate horizon, however, the sun does rise from the narrow gorge carved by the sacred Vilcanota River, which we have seen is linked with Ausangate (from behind which the December solstice rises), the Milky Way, the sun's passage, and water/fertility beliefs in general.

There is a unique stone carving located close to the Intimachay cave that has commonly been thought to represent a condor because of similarities between it and a condor's head (Figure 3.27). Bearing in mind that this identification is by no means certain, it might be recalled that we have already seen how condors are believed over much of the Andes to represent—or manifest—the mountain deities, including Salcantay.

TERRACES, IRRIGATION, AND FOUNTAINS

Machu Picchu is renowned for its terraces. It has been shown that terracing helps prevent erosion, increases the amount of level ground, and softens the effects of climatic variation.[193] This means that agricultural production is increased, especially as terraces are often irrigated, and thus the growing time is shortened.

The crop most likely cultivated at Machu Picchu was probably maize, with perhaps some potatoes.[194] Maize played an important role in religious ceremonies, and, given Machu Picchu's importance as a religious center, any grown at the site would have likely been viewed as especially sacred.

Mountain deities were (and still are) closely linked with cultivation terraces and irrigation systems,[195] and this was also the case in the Cuzco region.[196] This is understandable given their role in providing water and controlling the hydrological cycle,[197] the use made of their slopes,[198] and their perceived role in causing landslides and earthquakes.[199] It is, therefore, difficult to imagine the Incas not making offerings to the mountain on which they constructed terraces.

Figure 3.23. The rock inside the Sun Temple at Machu Picchu was carved to indicate the rise of the June solstice through the window opposite.

Figure 3.24. The Incas built the Sun Temple over a naturally formed cave.

Figure 3.25. The cave under the boulder of the Sun Temple was called the Royal Mausoleum by Bingham (although no funerary items were found), and the fine stonework inside it indicates that it had a ceremonial function. Here one sees the stepped, carved boulder at the entrance.

Figure 3.26. The so-called Temple of the Moon is a cave on the slopes of Huayna Picchu, which contains examples of some of fine Inca stonework.

Bingham noted the scarcity of water at Machu Picchu and even suggested that this lack may have been a reason for the abandonment of the site.[200] A recent hydrological study established, however, that the Incas did not abandon Machu Picchu because of water shortage.[201] We have seen how the water would have been considered sacred (Figures 3.28 and 3.29). A large number of well-built fountains is not common in Inca sites, and the ones at Machu Picchu probably were utilized in good part for ritual bathing and ablutions. This underscores the role that water played in the sacred nature of the site.

The extensive terracing and dominant position of Machu Picchu on a steep mountainside have led some people to point to what they believe is the excellent defensive nature of Machu Picchu (see Figure 3.30) .[202] Although Machu Picchu certainly is situated in an impressive location, there is no evidence that there was a serious threat from the jungle area, and recent analysis of bones found little cranial trauma, which suggests that the site did not experience attacks.[203] On one hand this evidence is consistent with the general picture we have of Machu Picchu's location being within a system of pilgrimage sites rather than ones of a defensive nature. On the other hand, as we will see, the Incas may have conquered the area, especially around Vitcos, west of Machu Picchu, at least in part to use as a base to attack their traditional enemies, the Chancas, in the hills to the west.[204]

Nonetheless, Machu Picchu seems to have been constructed primarily for religious reasons.[205] Scholars have noted that the walls and enclosures only hindered access rather than provided a solid system of defense. In some cases structures thought to have been defensive may have been built for other purposes (e.g., the moat likely was used to collect water runoff rather than to provide a defensive barrier). The outer walls seem to have been intended more for enclosing a religious site than for defense per se.[206] The idea that Machu Picchu was chosen for defensive reasons seems even less probable when we see that other important Inca centers in the area were not of a defensive nature.[207]

Figure 3.27. In the lower part of the photo is the so-called Condor Stone. The ruins above it are part of what Bingham called the Unusual Niches group.

Figure 3.28 (left). Water was routed from the lower right in this view north toward Machu Picchu from the northern slope of the mountain for which it is named.

Figure 3.29 (above). An enclosed fountain (bottom of photo) is the first in a series that descends from close to the Temple of the Sun. The fine stonework found in fountains and their locations at Machu Picchu suggest that they were used in rituals.

Figure 3.30. The construction of terraces on steep hillsides is one of the impressive aspects of Machu Picchu. View to the east from Cerro San Miguel.

Further Sites in the Region

Figure 4.1. Phuyupatamarka is at the origin of a river that joins the Urubamba River below and clearly was an important ceremonial site on the way to Machu Picchu.

If the construction of Machu Picchu was related to a significant degree to sacred landscape, it would seem likely that other sites associated with it would play supportive roles. They, too, might have features that could be better understood using our knowledge of sacred geography in the area. A discussion of these sites, some of which are quite important in their own right, will in turn enable us to see Machu Picchu within the broader context of which it was a part (see Figures 1.10 and 1.12).

PHUYUPATAMARKA

Phuyupatamarka is situated just below the crest of a ridge at approximately 3,550 m/11,647 feet elevation, ca. 6 km southeast of Machu Picchu. One of the most important sites along the famed Inca Trail (see Figure 1.12), it consists of structures that clearly formed part of a ceremonial complex (Figures 4.1 and 4.2).[208] Several "baths," probably used for ritual purposes, descend from a source that carries water originating from a spring in the mountainside.

About 100 m/328 feet above the main complex, on a high point of the ridge, is a platform with a retaining wall following the shape of the terrain. The platform affords excellent views of the major snowcapped peaks, including Salcantay to the south, numerous snow peaks (e.g., Pumasillo) to the west, and Veronica (Waqaywillka) to the east by northeast (see Figures 4.1, 4.3, and 4.4). Machu Picchu peak lies below to the north.

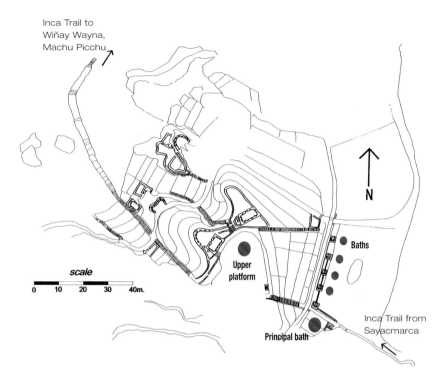

Figure 4.2. A plan of the ruins at Phuyupatamarka (adapted from MacLean 1986).

Although the summit platform could have served as a signal station, as suggested by some authors (e.g., the anthropologist Paul Fejos),[209] I believe its main function was as a place from which to worship the surrounding mountains. If the common custom at such sites was followed, then some of the ritual offerings would have been buried. This would explain why there was so much digging done there, and not apparently elsewhere, by treasure hunters. Of course, the place itself would have been sacred, this particular site doubtless having been chosen because of the water source, as the archaeologist Margaret MacLean has surmised.[210]

Water sources, especially those that led to important irrigation works, were usually considered sacred by the Incas. This source was likely perceived to have been related to Salcantay, being located on a ridge extending down from the mountain. Such beliefs are common throughout the Andes, as noted earlier. This connection with Salcantay would have increased the sacredness of the source of water and the summit platform associated with it.

The fact that no large structure exists on the summit should not lead one to assume that the hilltop itself was of minor importance. We know that most of the ritual sites on mountain summits were not impressive, whereas the mountains themselves were among the most important deities in Inca religion, and large complexes connected to their worship were frequently built on their slopes below.[211]

In summary, Phuyupatamarka was likely a pilgrimage site along the Inca Trail to Machu Picchu. The Inca sites along this road indicate it was a very sacred place because it was associated with an important water source and because it was a place where pilgrims could worship in view of the most sacred mountains of the region. Such worship would most likely have been for the usual reasons: fertility of crops and animals, protection of the people, success in trade, and so forth. This hypothesis helps explain the function of other aspects of the site as well, such as the ritual baths.

Figure 4.3. The arrow points to Pumasillo in the distance. A lone individual stands on the artificial platform above Phuyupatamarka.

Figure 4.4 A campsite at night near Phuyupatamarka with Veronica in the background.

WIÑAY WAYNA

The site of Wiñay Wayna (Huiñay Huayna) is situated down the slope from Phuyupatamarka and a couple of hours' walk southeast of Machu Picchu. It lies at an elevation of about 2,680 m/8,793 feet and is the last major complex of ruins on the Inca Trail before reaching Machu Picchu (see Figures 1.10, 1.12, and 4.5). It basically consists of two groups of structures, an upper and a lower, with a series of baths or fountains separating them, and some fine terracing (Figure 4.6).[212] Its religious character is indicated by its having nineteen fountains—more than any other Inca site.[213] Wiñay Wayna is near a waterfall that originates at Phuyupatamarka above (Figure 4.7), and the sites are linked by a superb section of Inca road. Thus it seems probable that, aside from assisting in food production (and possibly coca growing), Wiñay Wayna was built as a ritual stopping place along the pilgrimage road to Machu Picchu—with the sacred water as an important aspect of the site's function.[214]

Figure 4.5. View over ruins at Wiñay Wayna with Veronica in the background.

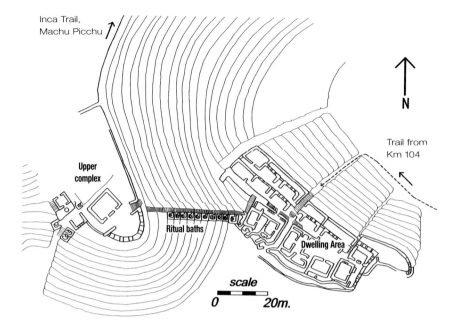

Figure 4.6. A plan of the ruins at Wiñay Wayna (adapted from MacLean 1986).

CHOQUESUYSUY, SAYACMARCA, RUNCU RACCAY, AND PIQUILLAKTA

Choquesuysuy, Sayacmarca (Sayacmarka), and Runcu Raccay illustrate the ritual importance of water (and in one case a hilltop) in complexes found on the same ridge (in the broadest sense) leading down from Salcantay. There are several other sites in this area, some of which have sacred elements (e.g., carved boulders), but they seem to have been more in the nature of support sites for Machu Picchu.[215]

Choquesuysuy lies just below a waterfall near a stream where it meets the Urubamba River a few kilometers upriver from Machu Picchu. This stream originates in the spring at Phuyupatamarka. A waterfall exists just above the site. As we would expect in view of what we have seen, Choquesuysuy has a sacred character, with fountains that likely played a role in the rituals performed there.[216]

Figure 4.7. View of ruins at Wiñay Wayna with a waterfall behind.

Sayacmarca and Runcu Raccay lie along the sacred road to Machu Picchu (Figures 1.10, 1.12, and 4.8), and they appear to have functioned in part as lodges and control points over roads.[217] They both, however, overlook the sources of rivers. In the case of Sayacmarca there is also a prominent, carved boulder at the site (see Figures 4.9 and 4.10). The main building of Runcu Raccay is formed by concentric circles of walls, which may be symbolic of a water cult—such circles being commonly interpreted elsewhere in the Andes in this way (Figures 4.11 and 4.12).[218] In what may be a reflection of a prehispanic custom, during the severe drought of 1988 men climbed up to the lake above the waterfall near Runcu Raccay and threw rocks into it to wake up the mythological being residing there in order for it to cause rain.[219] This was a practice at other sacred lakes during the Inca period.[220]

The popular hiking trail to Machu Picchu has as its traditional starting point the site of Pattallacta (also known as Llaktapata on some maps), an important site on the bank of the Urubamba River (Figure 4.13). The site likely supplied Machu Picchu with agricultural products grown in the area. It also has an important ceremonial sector, however, with a rare, elliptical wall surrounding a boulder

Figure 4.8. Trekkers follow the Inca Trail as it passes by lakes between Sayacmarca and Runcu Raccay.

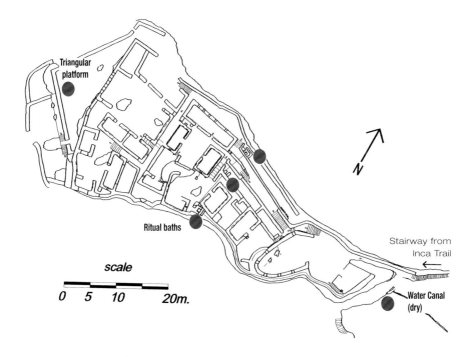

Figure 4.9. A plan of the ruins at Sayacmarca (Sayacmarka) (adapted from MacLean 1986).

situated directly above the Cusichaka (Kusichaca) River (Figure 4.14) close to its confluence with the Urubamba River (see Figure 4.15). Having examined ruins along the Inca Trail, I will now take a brief look at other sites near Machu Picchu that also appear to have played supportive and/or religious roles.

CERRO SAN MIGUEL

Across the Urubamba River from Machu Picchu to the west is a mountain called Cerro San Miguel (also Vizcachani) (ca. 2,924 m/9,593 feet) (see Figures 1.10 and 3.15). In 1989 Fernando Astete and I, along with other archaeologists from the National Institute of Culture, investigated an artificially formed circular platform on the mountain's summit. The platform is 25 m in diameter and has an upright stone in the center (Figure 4.16). All the principal sacred mountains of the region can be seen from this spot. The summit of San Miguel lies due west of

Figure 4.10. Ruins at Sayacmarca.

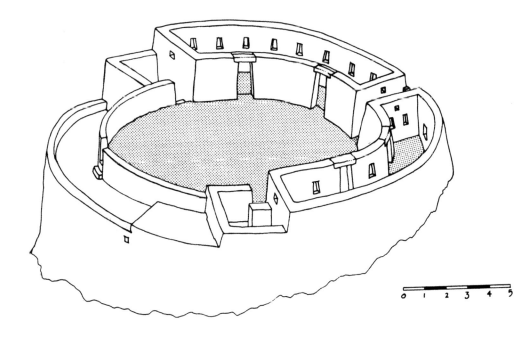

Figure 4.11. A plan of the principal structure Runcu Raccay (from MacLean 1986).

Figure 4.12. The main structure at Runcu Raccay.

Figure 4.13. An aerial view of Pattallacta, the site from which the Inca Trail traditionally begins.

Figure 4.14. The Pattallacta ceremonial complex has an elliptical wall, unusual for the Incas, which surrounds a boulder.

Machu Picchu. As viewed from the central stone, the Intihuatana is at 92° and the highest summit of Veronica at 91°; thus these two ritually significant landmarks are on the equinox line and in alignment with each other to one degree.

Parts of a well-constructed Inca road were also seen leading to the platform from the east side of the mountain up steep cliffs and through jungle, and this emphasizes the site's importance for the Incas. Farther along the San Miguel ridge to the north we saw small structures that are located at the point the June solstice would set (297°) as seen from the Intihuatana.[221] There seems little doubt that the platform with its central stone was constructed as a marker of the equinox, as a place to worship this combination of a mountaintop and sacred alignment, and, at least in part, for worship of the sacred geographical features on the horizon. It might be added that the mountain San Miguel is also surrounded, like Huayna Picchu, on three sides by the Urubamba River.

Figure 4.15. Trekkers on a trail that follows the south bank of the Urubamba River to Patallacta.

Figure 4.16. An elongated stone was found in the center of a circular platform on Cerro San Miguel's summit lying due west (the equinox line) from Machu Picchu. Salcantay is to the left in the background and the Quishuar range to the right.

LLAKTAPATA AND PALCAY

Bingham located the ruins of Llaktapata (ca. 2,760 m/9,055 feet) on a ridge between the Aobamba and Santa Teresa Rivers southwest of Machu Picchu.[222] In previous editions of this book I noted that little was known about Llaktapata (Llactapata) and that it did not seem to have had any particular ceremonial function. (12) Scholars thought that it was likely to have been a control point and clearing house for goods. Given its location, however, in a setting similar to Machu Picchu's, I thought that further research needed to be undertaken to determine its possible function.

This research was provided by McKim Malville, Hugh Thomson, and Gary Ziegler, who investigated Llaktapata in 2003. They surveyed more than 80 structures, divided into five sectors. While documenting the orientations of the structures, they discovered striking parallels with my findings at Machu Picchu and also similarities in orientation, design, and scale of buildings in Sector 1 with the Temple of the Sun (Coricancha) in Cuzco. For example, a structure they designated as the "Sun Temple" had the outward extension of its corridors align with sunrise over Machu Picchu at the June solstice. Among other alignments, they noted that the sight line between the Priest's House at Machu Picchu (open to the December solstice sunset and Pumasillo) and the Llaktapata Sun Temple function in diametrically opposite directions for both solstices and mountains (see Figure 4.17). A large, artificially raised platform (*usnu* or *ushnu*) aligns with the December solstice sunrise. They located small platforms on crags that lie directly on the equinox line as it crosses the summit of Cerro San Miguel (with its Intihuatana-like stone), and thus the line extends on via Machu Picchu's Intihuatana and Mount Veronica. They noted other solstice and mountain alignments and also that several structures and a central plaza were aligned with the cardinal directions.

Figure 4.17. A plan showing the alignments of Llaktapata with Machu Picchu (from Malville, Thomson, and Ziegler 2004).

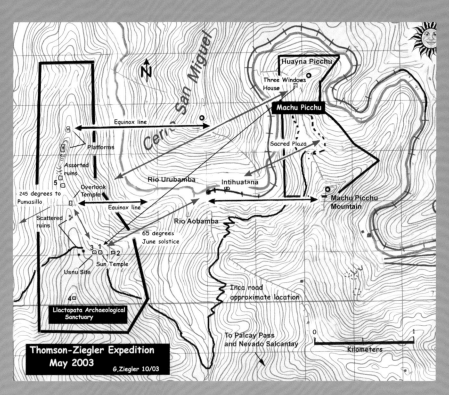

Their findings suggest an intent to achieve mutually interactive sight lines, and they observe, "Solstice-equinox orientation in relationship with alignments on Huayna Picchu and Mount Machu Picchu indicates that adoration and ritual focus on these special mountains and the sun may have been the primary purpose at Llaktapata." They conclude: "The sightlines, shrines, and buildings of Machu Picchu and Llaktapata appear to establish an extended ritual neighborhood of Machu Picchu, containing geographical, astronomical, and cosmological meaning" (see Figure 4.17).[223]

In 1985 I located a section of Inca road that ran up from the Llaktapata ruins along the eastern side of the ridge. (13) The ridge extends from Salcantay via the peak called Tucarhuay and parallels the one on which Machu Picchu lies (see Figures 1.10 and 4.18). The two ridges are separated by the Aobamba River, but they are connected via a series of trails. Bingham followed a trail on the western side of the Llaktapata ridge before it descended to the Palcay ruins, at the headwaters of the Aobamba River. This caused him to miss the eastern trail and sites that I located higher along the ridge.

We found an interesting group of structures on a knoll at 3,567 m (11,703 feet) at the edge of the tree line. The Incas had constructed two well-built structures enclosed by a low wall that curves around one end. Next to it is a boulder with carved steps (Figures 4.19 and 4.20).[224] The site's architecture and location

Figure 4.18. A campsite near the pass east of Salcantay on the trail to Palcay.

Figure 4.19. Measuring the height of a wall inside one of the ruins located on the ridge above Llaktapata at 3,507 m (11,506 feet).

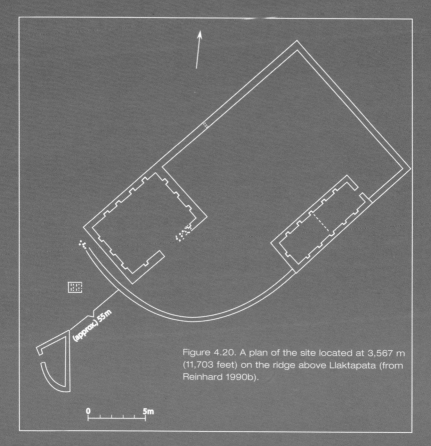

Figure 4.20. A plan of the site located at 3,567 m (11,703 feet) on the ridge above Llaktapata (from Reinhard 1990b).

Figure 4.21. Men at lower right follow an Inca trail as it ascends diagonally through a cliff above the site in Figure 4.20.

suggest that it primarily served a ceremonial function. The trail continued on, partly cut through the side of a cliff, connecting Llaktapata with Palcay (Figures 4.21 and 4.22).

The Inca site at Palcay (ca. 3,340 m/10,958 feet) was probably important, at least in part, for economic and strategic reasons.[225] It is situated at the junction of trails that link Machu Picchu with important Inca sites: Tarawasi to the south and Llaktapata and the Santa Teresa River (and eventually the sites of the Vilcabamba region) to the west (Figures 1.10 and 4.23). The site, however, may have had a religious role as well. It is located below a waterfall at the confluence of rivers originating in the glaciers of the sacred mountains Salcantay and Tucarhuay (Figure 4.24). Two of the four rooms are well built, but the others were not completed before the site was abandoned. There is, however, a clear division into what would have been four identical rooms aligned precisely with the cardinal directions (Figure 4.25).[226] Its association with Salcantay and a river flowing north from it may not be coincidental, especially in view of the orientations and locations of other sites in the region, as we have seen.

The archaeological complexes located within the region all appear to either have played roles of support or to have had ceremonial functions that complemented Machu Picchu. Together they formed an elaborate pilgrimage system, with Machu Picchu as its center.[227] All of the sites show in their construction and placement a great concern with adaptation to the natural landscape. In some important cases they demonstrate a close association with sacred geographical features, which in turn are aligned with astronomical events of special significance to the Incas. Although more research is needed, the evidence from this examination of the outlying sites suggests that the Incas were intent on accomplishing a feat that demonstrates an extraordinary vision—the physical integration of a wide variety of sites, with their cosmology writ large over a vast, sacred landscape.

Figure 4.22. Part of the trail shown in Figure 4.21 was carved through solid rock.

Figure 4.23. An Inca trail cuts horizontally across a sheer cliff on the side of Machu Picchu Mountain. It linked the site of Machu Picchu with Palcay and Llaktapata.

Figure 4.24. The upper region of the Aobamba River where the ruins of Palcay are located.

Figure 4.25. A plan of an unfinished Inca complex at Palcay (adapted from Bingham 1913).

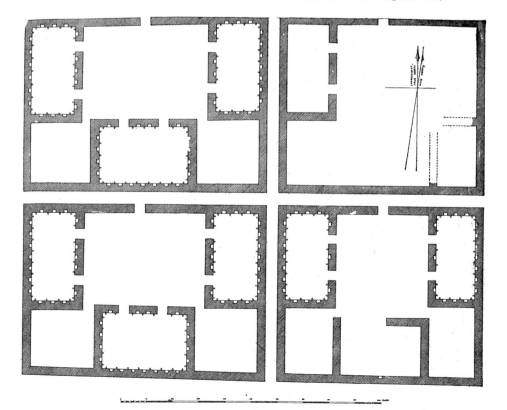

Chapter Five

The Builders of Machu Picchu

The identification of those primarily responsible for the construction of Machu Picchu could offer clues to its purpose. Some writers have speculated that parts of the site had been constructed a couple of hundred years before the Spanish conquest.[228] Given that the region was inhabited to some degree prior to the Incas,[229] it would not be surprising to find some evidence of pre-Inca use of the ridge at Machu Picchu.[230] Based on a study of the architecture and archaeological remains, however, the site visible today has been thought by the majority of Inca scholars to date to the time of the expansion of the Inca Empire during the reigns of Pachacuti and Topa Inca, during the second half of the fifteenth century.[231]

Figure 5.1. A man representing the emperor Pachacuti is carried at the festival of Inti Raymi in Cuzco.

In 1987 the archaeologist John Rowe discussed a sixteenth-century document that indicates that Machu Picchu was an estate of Pachacuti Inca Yupanqui.[232] Pachacuti has been credited with the initial expansion of the Inca Empire outside of the Cuzco valley and into the Vilcabamba region, where he established a center at Vitcos in the mid-1400s (Figures 1.10 and 5.1).[233]

Of interest from the perspective of sacred geography is that Pachacuti was likely responsible for the construction, or at least improvement, of a number of sites associated with mountain worship (e.g., on Pachatusan, Walla Walla, and Huanacauri), as well as numerous ceremonial complexes where worship of sacred geographical features took place. He is also the emperor who reportedly had Cuzco rebuilt to better reflect political-religious-economic concepts and ensured its establishment as a sacred center in the Andean world.[234]

Among the many projects Pachacuti is credited with undertaking is the elaboration of the *ceque* system, a series of imaginary lines radiating out from the Temple of the Sun in Cuzco, which had more than 330 *huacas* (sacred places or objects) situated along them (Figure 5.2).[235] The anthropologist David Gow found that stones, mountains, and water sources made up 68 percent of these huacas.[236] The ceques were themselves closely tied to the distribution of water in

Figure 5.2. A diagram of the ceque (imaginary line) system at Cuzco (from Bauer 1998).

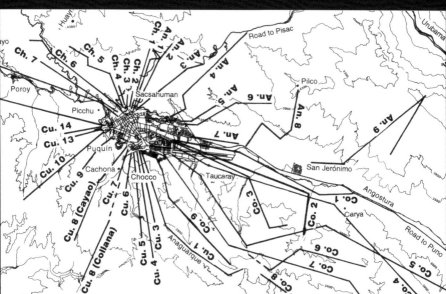

Figure 5.3. The ruins of Pisac, a royal estate of the emperor Pachacuti, who abandoned it and went on to build Machu Picchu.

the Cuzco valley.[237] This concern with the sacred geographical environment continued with Pachacuti's son, Topa Inca, during whose reign (ca. AD 1463–1493) hundreds of ceremonial sites were constructed on mountain summits throughout the Andes.[238]

According to Rowe, Pachacuti undertook the conquest of Vilcabamba in order to use it as a base for attacking his enemies, the Chancas.[239] He may have established Machu Picchu as a memorial to his conquest. The archaeologist Ann Kendall believes that Pachacuti might have intended it to be a ceremonial center to replace the important site of Pisac (northeast of Cuzco), which he had built and later abandoned (Figure 5.3).[240]

During Pachacuti's Vilcabamba campaign Machu Picchu could have been of more strategic importance.[241] Cobo wrote of how the native people of Vilcabamba were impressed by constructions undertaken by the Incas and how this was a reason they eventually submitted to them.[242] Surely the construction of sites and roads throughout the rugged region would have served to demonstrate Inca dominance to the local inhabitants.

The emphasis on religion would also have been linked to such dominance, since the deities would have controlled the economy and protected the people of the region. When the Amaybamba Valley was later conquered, it became the preferred route into Vilcabamba and the road that passed near Machu Picchu fell into disuse.[243] After the Incas rose up against the Spaniards but were defeated at Cuzco, they retreated and established their capital at Vitcos (Figure 5.4).

As we have seen, mountain worship was closely linked with weather control, and mountain deities were often protector deities of regions they dominated. In this regard it is interesting that Pachacuti chose as his guardian "brother" deity Illapa, the weather god. He took a statue of Illapa with him to war.[244] The association of weather gods (often mountain deities) and war was widespread at that time in the Andes[245] and still is today.[246] Illapa was probably utilized by the state to incorporate the regional weather gods under one generalized deity.[247]

In any event Pachacuti's selection of Illapa as his "brother" deity demonstrates his concern with having a close relationship with a weather/war god. An important religious center such as Machu Picchu, constructed in good part for worship of

Figure 5.4. The Spanish destroyed much of the Inca capital of Vitcos, and only a few entranceways remained intact.

mountain, weather, and protector deities in a region he had conquered, would accord with Inca beliefs in general and with Pachacuti's actions in particular.

John Rowe noted that if Machu Picchu was one of Pachacuti's estates, it fell outside the administrative system of the Inca Empire.[248] Instead, it came under the jurisdiction of the group (*panaca*) composed of his direct descendants except for his successor, the next Inca emperor.[249] Machu Picchu is unusual among the estates of emperors, however, in that it has an elaborate series of sites with important ritual components built on along a defined pilgrimage route, now known as the Inca Trail.

Recent studies undertaken with the Bingham collection at Yale have added support to the idea of Machu Picchu having been an estate, uncovering evidence of a diverse population with a variety of goods brought in from great distances. Scholars disagree, however, about whether Machu Picchu could be considered an actual "estate." Part of the problem may lie in the difficulty of having an Inca concept agree with its English (or Spanish) gloss. There appears to have been considerable variety among the different "estates" associated with even a single Inca emperor. For example, Pachacuti built estates at Pisac and Ollantaytambo that differ from Machu Picchu, not least in the latter being part of an elaborate system of connected sites (e.g., Phuyupatamarka, Sayacmarca, Wiñay Wayna). Rather than each one of these Inca Trail sites being a separate "estate," they were deliberately constructed in relation to Machu Picchu and should be viewed as parts of a whole. There are other differences as well. Unlike Machu Picchu, for example, most estates do not have large plazas. In any event the pilgrimage aspect of Machu Picchu makes it clear that if it is to be called an "estate," it differed significantly from others known to historians. (14)

If Machu Picchu was maintained in the same way as other estates, its abandonment could have been due in part to the *panaca* having found it difficult to continue the maintenance of the sites. This would have especially been the case once the civil war began between the brothers Atahualpa and Huascar, which followed the death of the emperor Huayna Capac sometime around 1527.

In the original study of the skeletons found in burials at Machu Picchu, a high percentage of female skeletons (approximately 4:1, females to males) was reported.[250] This led Hiram Bingham to conclude that it had been a home for the Virgins of the Sun. The maintenance of an isolated estate, however, along with departure of men for the war between Atahualpa and Huascar (and later battles with the Spaniards), could have explained such a high female-to-male ratio, assuming that it existed. In addition, there had long been some doubt that the gender of the bones had been correctly identified, and recently it has been established that the supposed gender imbalance was actually about 1.54:1 (females to males).[251]

Bingham's hypothesis that Machu Picchu was a home for the Virgins of the Sun was further weakened by the meagerness of the artifacts found in the burials.[252] One would expect more elaborate burials in the cases of high-status females.

Bingham's hypothesis had also been influenced by his identification of Machu Picchu as Vilcabamba the Old, the last capital of the Incas.[253] This opinion is no longer shared by the vast majority of scholars, who instead have identified Vilcabamba the Old at the place now called Espiritu Pampa, located deeper in the jungle (Figure 5.5).[254]

Other sites in the region of Machu Picchu formed parts of a system of roads and buildings that linked Cuzco with Vilcabamba, and these were also abandoned at the same time. Therefore, it appears likely that this was part of a deliberate policy to leave the area unpopulated and isolated.[255] This remote region would have served as a rugged buffer zone to prevent Spanish incursions into the area, which a document of 1562 clearly indicates.[256] According to this document, Tupac Amaru and his brother Titu Cusi reportedly "pillaged and burned all the Indian houses of the *repartimientos* [land divisions] of Amaybamba and Picchu." This would help explain the mystery of why Machu Picchu was abandoned and why it remained relatively intact (minus objects of real value to the Incas) and undiscovered for such a long time. (15)

Figure 5.5. A reconstruction of what the Incas' last capital of Vilcabamba (Espiritu Pampa) would have looked like at the time of Inca occupation (from Lee 2000).

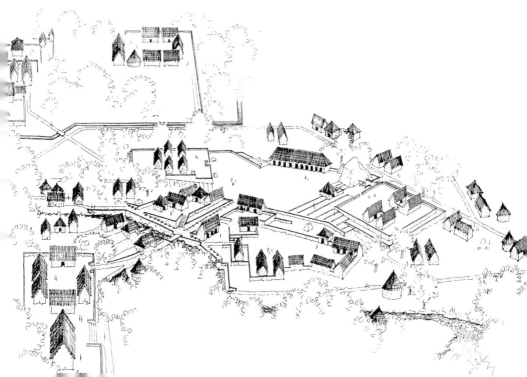

Chapter Six

Conclusions: The Sacred Center

Figure 6.1. An annual pilgrimage is made during the festival of Qoyllur Riti to glaciers on the slopes of Mount Qolquepunku, east of Cuzco. Traditional beliefs associate the worship there as being principally for

As we have seen, a large and complex set of factors would have contributed to Machu Picchu's economic, political, and religious importance, and I will summarize only a few of the principal ones here. Machu Picchu may have been a royal retreat built partly to commemorate Pachacuti's successful campaign against the Chancas.[257] Some scholars believe that Machu Picchu was an important site because of its strategic economic and political situation between the forest lowlands and Cuzco.[258] It would have helped control trade and provided security to farmers in the fertile nearby valleys.[259] Perhaps Machu Picchu was itself a center for communities that grew warm-weather crops such as coca leaves and maize.[260] Although these factors would have affected the growth and importance of Machu Picchu, they still do not seem to explain its inaccessible location or its religious significance.

A careful look at the geographical location of Machu Picchu reveals that it is not only at an ecological center between the mountain highlands and the forest lowlands, but it is also located among the most sacred mountains of the region. In addition, it is virtually encircled by the sacred Urubamba River, which flows generally in a southeast to northwest direction, replicating the passage of the sun. At key times of the Inca calendar the sun rises and sets behind snowcapped mountains, which are still considered powerful deities today. The Southern Cross, center of the Milky Way, the celestial river in Inca thought, lies in juxtaposition with Salcantay, one of the most sacred mountains of the Incas and directly connected to Machu Picchu. Sacred mountains lie in the four cardinal directions from the site. This central location of Machu Picchu, itself built on a mountain, recalls the discussion by Mircea Eliade of the importance of an *axis mundi* in world religions.[261] The axis mundi becomes a sacred center conceptually uniting the earth and sky. Whatever the Incas believed, they would have been aware of the central position of Machu Picchu in relation to the mountains, and major ceremonies at Machu Picchu would certainly have involved mountain worship.

We know that mountain worship preceded the Incas.[262] There is also evidence indicating that the concept of a center surrounded by four sacred mountains was a pre-Inca one: both the Wari (Huari) and Tiahuanaco cultures (which arose during the first millennium AD) appear to have developed within this conceptual, physical scheme.[263] Given our understanding of the reasons why mountains were so important to the Incas, it is clear that they would have been seen as protectors and as providers of economic stability. When actual mountains coincided closely with important celestial phenomena and the cardinal directions, the sacredness of the place in the center would surely have increased.

The region of Machu Picchu appears to have been part of a larger system centered in Cuzco. I have referred to the association, both physical and conceptual, between the principal mountains of the greater Cuzco region, Salcantay and Ausangate. It is beyond the scope of this book to detail the sacred geography of the Cuzco Valley (or the Vilcanota Valley system with which it is connected), but I would like to make brief reference to it in order to help place Machu Picchu within the larger cosmological and sacred geographical system of the Incas.

The important role played by Salcantay at Machu Picchu has been examined previously, and I would only add that Cuzco lies near a midpoint between Salcantay and Ausangate along a line that runs southeast-northwest. Thus it is in accord with the flow of the Vilcanota (Urubamba) River, the route of the deity Viracocha (as we saw in Chapter Two), and the sun's passage during an important part of the year—the time of rains and the growth of crops and herds (see Figure 2.4).

Cuzco also lies near a water divide. It is at the source of a river that flows southeast into the Vilcanota River, which in turn flows northwest. Cuzco is situated on the eastern side of the water divide with a direct view of Ausangate, which still is the center for mountain worship in the region east of Cuzco (see Figures 2.3, 2.4, and 6.1). Cuzco is also located just below a pass that provides a view of Salcantay (Figure 6.2). Senqa, one of the mountains on the northwestern border of the Cuzco Valley, was believed to be the direct origin of the water that passed through Cuzco and also was perceived to have brought rain from the sky.[264] Cuzco was thus at the symbolic center for a circulation of waters,[265] in addition to being a center for the most powerful sacred mountains of the greater Cuzco region.

Figure 6.2. The pyramid-shaped, snowcapped mountain is Salcantay. This picture was taken from near the pass that lies directly above Cuzco to the west. Cuzco is located between Salcantay and Ausangate, two of the most important geographical features in the Cuzco region.

Machu Picchu, built by Pachacuti (the emperor responsible for establishing Cuzco as a symbolic center for the Andean world), surely would have been seen as a prominent sacred center. It was within a sacred geographical subsystem, as it were, with Salcantay, one end of the larger system, serving as its principal focus. Despite its remoteness, the area was of great importance economically, religiously, and politically for the Inca Empire. Machu Picchu would have been an important pilgrimage destination for the conqueror of the region, Pachacuti, and his descendants. Special offerings would have been made to state deities, such as the sun, and to those believed associated with key sacred geographical features, especially mountains. Abandonment of the site and extensive looting have left us with only a fragmentary record of what these offerings would have involved. Finds made at Machu Picchu, however—and at less disturbed ceremonial sites elsewhere in the empire—suggest that these would have included sacrifices of llamas and offerings of high-status items of textiles, ceramics, and statues (Figures 6.3, 6.4, and 6.5). (16)

Given the above, an examination of the sacred geographies at other Inca ceremonial sites would seem essential for better understanding the reasons for their locations and their functions. This approach has already proven useful in interpreting pre-Inca ceremonial complexes as well.[266]

What I have attempted to do in this book is demonstrate the ways in which Machu Picchu fits into a sacred geographical setting and how understanding this can help us in interpreting the significance of its location and its primary functions. The distribution and types of sacred stones, the astronomical alignments of many of the structures, the ways that symbolic and functional elements of Cuzco may have been replicated at the site, and the relationship of the sites in the region to each other are only some of the more obvious areas that need further investigation.

Nonetheless, I am confident that further research will not change the basic concept of Machu Picchu as a site built in a location selected in large part because of the sacred geographical features surrounding it. These features have been found to be closely associated with some of the most important aspects of Inca life: the fertility of crops and animals, political control, empowerment of ritual specialists, trade, and the hydrological cycle as it interacts with the celestial sphere.

Our knowledge of Inca religion indicates that worship of major (nonmountain) deities such as Viracocha, Illapa, and Inti (the sun) certainly would have taken place at the site. But the reasons for Machu Picchu's location and the key to much of its meaning appear clearly to be associated with the sacred geography of the region. At Machu Picchu we find a unique combination of landscape and cosmological beliefs that together formed a powerful sacred center uniting religion, economics, and politics. These factors led to the construction of one of the most impressive ceremonial sites of the ancient world.

Figure 6.4. A male tunic from a mountain ceremonial site on Llullaillaco illustrates the colorful and fine quality work of Inca textiles.

Figure 6.3: This model of the Ice Maiden found on Mount Ampato illustrates the dress of an Inca noble woman (courtesy of Christopher Klein).

Figure 6.5. Male and female Inca statues found on Mount Llullaillaco have miniature clothing similar to that worn by adult Inca nobles.

Recent Research in the Machu Picchu Region

Although the first edition of this book appeared in 1991, I found little in the text that needed changing while preparing this latest edition. Several publications relating to Machu Picchu and other sites in the Vilcabamba region have added information of interest. A number of guidebooks have appeared, and Ruth Wright and Alfredo Valencia (2001) have provided one, *The Machu Picchu Guidebook*, that stands out for its thoroughness and pictorial documentation. Fine summaries of the Machu Picchu Historical Sanctuary are those of Frost (1995) and Kauffmann-Doig (2005).

Figure E.2. Restoration work in the "Industrial Group."

Archaeological studies include an important volume by Valencia and Gibaja (1992) that has a compilation of excavations undertaken at the site over several years. One of the most significant investigations undertaken in recent years was the hydrological study of the site by Kenneth Wright and Alfredo Valencia (2000). In addition to demonstrating the flow of water through Machu Picchu, they located the remains of an Inca trail connecting the site with the Urubamba River, established that the Incas did not have to abandon Machu Picchu because of a water shortage, and estimated that 60 percent of the work that went into the site's construction lies underground (Wright and Valencia 2000:19–24, 38). Richard Burger and Lucy Salazar (2003 and 2004) edited two volumes with articles reanalyzing the Machu Picchu materials recovered by Bingham (see Burger 2004; Miller 2003; Niles 2004; Verano 2003). The aforementioned books are essential reading for any serious scholar interested in Machu Picchu.

Studies focusing on new interpretative material directly relating to Machu Picchu are few (see the list of publications in Programa Machu Picchu 2000). There are some that remain within the range of possibility given our understanding of Andean

gure E.1. A view across the main plaza to the eastern sector of Machu Picchu, called by Bingham
ie "Industrial Group." Much of the recent restoration work undertaken at the site has taken place in
is sector.

135

beliefs (albeit with some imaginative leaps [e.g., Sánchez 1989]). Others have little basis in historical, ethnographic, or archaeological facts (e.g., Westerman 1998). Ironically, in view of my own focus on the importance of sacred mountains, some guides at the ruins now describe stones as representing mountains, even when there is little to support this beyond their having pointed shapes—hardly convincing in itself. Wright and Valencia (2000:8, 13), however, added some intriguing examples of "arrow stones" (i.e., triangles carved in stones that point in the direction of major peaks) and stones mimicking the shapes of mountains in the distance. Gary Ziegler and Kim Malville (2003) have provided additional evidence of the importance of solstice and mountain alignments at Machu Picchu.

The most noticeable changes at Machu Picchu have been in the physical realm, especially the restoration projects (Figures E.1 and E.2) and the opening of a site museum, the Museo de Sitio Manuel Chávez Ballón—Machu Picchu (Astete 2005). There have also been changes in the modern-day cultural sphere (Figure E.3). For example, there has been a considerable expansion in the role played by what has been called "mystic tourism" (Flores 1996 and 2004) (Figure E.4). Machu Picchu has come to be seen as a place of special power and attracts New

Figure E.3. A folk dance in the Sacred Plaza at Machu Picchu.

Agers and Andean mystics alike. Several books have appeared that describe mystical experiences (Cumes and Lizárraga 1999; Wilcox 1999; see also Barrionuevo 2000) and initiations at Machu Picchu (Jenkins 1997). It is likely that these activities will continue to grow.

Recent excavations at or near Machu Picchu have been few and limited in scope (see Valencia 2004). In 2001 the archaeologist Fernando Astete led a team to the summit of Yanantin, a mountain that stands out across from Machu Picchu to the northeast. As was described in the text, Yanantin appears to have played an important symbolic role at Machu Picchu. Although no ruins were found on its summit (quite difficult to access), remains of more Inca roadwork were discovered nearby (Fernando Astete, personal communication 2002). Kaupp and Fernández (1999) found a ceremonial platform at the pass of Chaskaqasa (close to Yanantin), and Kaupp and Rodriguez (2004) described ceremonial sites associated with the mountain Veronica above the northern side of the Urubamba River.

In the Vilcabamba region, to the west of Machu Picchu, several discoveries of archaeological sites have been made in recent years. Within view of Machu Picchu the site of Llaktapata (Llactapata) on the ridge between the Aobamba and Santa Teresa rivers (see chapter 4) was more thoroughly investigated by McKim Malville, Hugh Thomson, and Gary Ziegler (2004). As noted previously, they discovered remarkable similarities at the site to the findings I have presented about Machu Picchu.

Vincent Lee (2000) has presented a summary of his years of research still farther west, and he identifies (in some cases for the first time) most of the sites noted in the chronicles of this region. Robert von Kaupp has led several trips into the area, and his reports have described several previously unknown sites (see Kaupp and Delgado 2001; Kaupp and Fernández 1997, 1999, and 2000; Kaupp and Rodriguez 2004). Gary Ziegler has located a number of sites in the Vilcabamba, and he, Peter Frost, and Alfredo Valencia have led teams that discovered Inca ruins north of the important ceremonial center of Choquequirao (Frost 2004; Ziegler 2001). This latter site was what first generated Bingham's interest in searching for the lost capital of Vilcabamba the Old and thus led to his discovery of Machu Picchu. It has been extensively cleared and restored during the past decade (see Figure 1.11).

Although it is not my intention to cite all of the publications that have recently appeared relating to the Incas, there are a few that might be mentioned for the complementary role they have relative to issues noted in this book. Susan Niles's (1999) book on Inca royal estates makes for interesting comparative material for any study of Machu Picchu. Brian Bauer and David Dearborn (1995) have published an excellent overview of Inca astronomy. This is especially important to read in conjunction with Bauer's (1998) book on the system of conceptual

Figure E.4. A painting with mystical allusions greets visitors near the entrance to Machu Picchu.

lines (*ceques*) that linked more than 300 sacred sites at Cuzco. Bauer and Stanish (2001) wrote about Inca pilgrimage and ceremonial complexes at Lake Titicaca, and their book provides valuable material to compare with Machu Picchu and adjacent sites. To this might be added my own studies of an Inca underwater ritual site in Lake Titicaca (Reinhard 1992b) and Inca pilgrimage centers in other parts of the empire (Astete and Reinhard 2003; Reinhard 1992a, 1992c, 1995, 1996, 1997, 1998a, 1998b, 1998c, 1999a, 1999b, 2005; Reinhard and Ceruti 2000, 2005, 2006, n.d.). Indeed, it was in part thanks to my work at Machu Picchu that I began to search for these sites because of their apparent relationship with significant features of the sacred landscape.

ARCHAEOLOGICAL THEORY AND SACRED LANDSCAPE STUDIES

Since I first began gathering information about Machu Picchu in the early 1980s, there have been significant advances made that involve archaeological theory and what has come to be called "landscape archaeology"—especially its symbolic and sacred aspects. There is an increased realization that "all societies in the past would have recognized, as do all societies in the present, some features of their landscapes . . . as sacred" (Ucko 1994: xix). Several studies, mainly in Europe, have demonstrated that archaeological sites need to be placed within the broader context of physical and sacred features of the landscape—particularly one dominated by mountains (see, e.g., Ashmore and Knapp 1999; Bender 1993; Carmichael et al. 1994; Hirsch and O'Hanlon 1995; Tilley 1994; Ucko and Layton 1999).

Nonetheless, archaeologists have only recently begun applying this approach to prehispanic sites located in the dramatic topography of the Andes. Research undertaken in recent years has shown that the meanings not only of Inca, but also of pre-Inca, ceremonial sites can be better understood when they are examined using the perspective of sacred landscape (see Bauer 1998; Bauer and Stanish 2001; Guchte 1990; Heffernan 1991, 1996; Hyslop 1990; Kolata and Ponce 1992; Niles 1992; Reindel 1999; Zapata 1998). In my particular case I have applied this perspective to some of the most enigmatic sites in the Andes, including Chavín, Tiahuanaco, and the giant drawings called the Nazca Lines (see Reinhard 1985b, 1987, 1988, 1990a, 1992b, 1992d, 2002).

The examination of Machu Picchu's association with sacred mountains allows it to be placed within this ever-widening body of studies and thus permits comparisons to be made that advance our understanding of cultural adaptations. Since research about a cultural landscape always involves an element of interpretation, it especially fits in with recent theoretical approaches, above all those that fall under the label "post-processual" or "interpretative" (see Hodder 1999:5; Johnson 1999:98–107; Shanks and Hodder 1998). One thing that characterizes "interpretative" archaeology when compared to other archaeological approaches is "much more importance being placed upon symbolism and other cognitive factors" (Dark 1995:10). Thus, a materialist (or "processual") interpretation of landscape stresses the practical importance of the resources it supplies and therefore that it is a commodity to be exploited (cf. Johnson 1999:103). The interpretative approach would take this into account but would focus more on the ways that the landscape is perceived and the kinds of interaction that take place between it and the culture in which it is embedded.

As we have seen, Machu Picchu was an important place of pilgrimage. The concept of landscape is an especially powerful organizing metaphor for examining pilgrimage cross-culturally and through time (Coleman and Elsner 1995:212). The Incas demonstrated the importance of sacred landscape features through the construction of ceremonial centers in or near them and the establishment of state-sponsored pilgrimages (Reinhard and Ceruti 2006, n.d.). In the end this resulted in one of the most awesome achievements in the prehistory of the Andes—the construction of Machu Picchu in one of the world's most rugged and spectacular landscapes.

Appendix

Cardinal Directions and Sacred Mountains

In the main body of the text I described the role that cardinal directions appear to have played in the conceptual organization of Machu Picchu. Because some scholars have doubted that north and south played a role in Inca thought, I decided to add a few words on the subject.

The importance of the cardinal directions of east and west has long been known in Inca studies (Rowe 1946:300). They have an obvious linkage with the rising and setting points of the sun at the times of the equinoxes, something of no small significance to a people among whom sun worship figured so prominently. East, in particular, has been one of the most important directions for Andean peoples, due to its being the direction of the rising sun (see Tschopik 1951:253), which in turn is associated with fertility (Riviere 1982:191). Garcilaso (1966 [1609]:117, 413; 1967 [1609] 1:120) was apparently the only chronicler to note directly the importance of the equinoxes, and some scholars have doubted his reliability on this point. Zuidema (1988:154–156), however, has demonstrated that there is indirect evidence provided by other chroniclers of their importance, especially with regard to the September equinox.

The Incas were also concerned with duality and oppositions, dual social and political divisions turning into quadripartitions, as was the case in Cuzco itself (Rostworowski 1983; Wachtel 1973). Although there are many exceptions, which are to be expected given the fact that cardinal directions would constitute only one among several factors taken into account for orientating sites (Zuidema 1986), numerous ceremonial structures in Inca and pre-Inca times had their sides aligned with the cardinal directions (see Beorchia 1985 for Inca ritual structures on mountain summits; Ponce 1989:93 for Tiahuanaco sites; Rowe 1967:97 for the nearly 3,000-year-old ceremonial center at Chavín de Huantar).

Figure A.1. A view to the east over the Inca ceremonial site on the summit of Pachatusan, the highest mountain bordering the Cuzco Valley. The Ausangate massif is visible in the distance.

Of course, square and rectangular structures in an east-west alignment would have all sides running in cardinal directions. But this is precisely the point: Andean peoples would not ignore that directions were formed in direct opposition to the sacred east-west ones, even assuming they made no attempt to establish these directions through astronomical observations (see Urton 1978:162–164 for how this positioning could have been done). That something more was involved than a simple play of oppositions is suggested by the current-day belief near Cuzco that two enormous mountains stand at the northern and southern boundaries of the earth (Urton 1981:36). I have also observed in current-day rituals in several areas of the Andes that offerings are made in the cardinal directions as a way of insuring the "completeness" of a ceremony. Not only has this been reported elsewhere in the Andes (see, e.g., Buechler and Buechler 1971:95), but cardinal directions were also involved in the organization of villages and social groups and in turn were connected with ceremonial sites, including those on mountains (Riviere 1982:164, 170, 190–191).

The Incas conceptually divided Cuzco and the rest of their empire into four (*tawantin*) regions (*suyus*), hence the term *Tawantinsuyu* for the Inca Empire. The lines dividing the four regions extended out from the Temple of the Sun, and they were perceived to ideally extend in the cardinal directions (Zuidema 1986:189). According to Zuidema (1986:189–193), however, only the one to the west actually did so. The others deviated because of local factors, principally relating to the hydrological system.

Thus, the east line followed the course of the Huatanay River as it flowed out of Cuzco (Zuidema 1986:189–190). If a compass reading is taken from the Coricancha (Temple of the Sun), the center for the *ceque* (imaginary line) system, then it has an azimuth of approximately 110° (see Figure 5.2). If this line was to extend to the far horizon, it would be in the direction both of the mountain Ausangate and the December solstice sunrise (111°).

From a map showing the division into the four *suyus* (Zuidema 1986:182), it can be seen that the eastern line is even farther south than 110° and that, if extended, this line would exclude Ausangate from that *suyu*. We know, however, that Ausangate was one of the most important sacred places of Collasuyu (Guaman Poma 1956 [1613]:196). Therefore, it seems possible that the line either kept to the 110° bearing, which would be in keeping with Zuidema's original statement (plus follow the example of the southern line, as we will see below) and that the map is wrong, or that it might even have returned to a due east direction once it left the immediate vicinity of Cuzco, which was as far as the *ceque* lines noted by Cobo (1964 [1653]; 1990 [1653]) extended.

It might be added that if the eastern line did lead due east, there was still an association with sacred mountains. The rising sun at that time came up from behind

Pachatusan, albeit just to the right of the highest summit. Pachatusan was noted as being sacred at the time of the Incas (see Santa Cruz Pachacuti 1968 [1571]:299, 305; Rendon 1960:117) and continues to be a powerful local mountain god to the present day (Sallnow 1987:129–130), worshipped as a source of fertility for crops and livestock (Pedro Quispe, personal communication 1987). Archaeological remains support its importance in Inca times. Ceremonial structures (artificial platforms and buildings with fine stonework built into cliff sides) are situated high on the mountain, including at the point where the equinox line crosses it as seen from the Temple of the Sun (Astete and Reinhard 2003; Rendon 1960:117) (Figure A.1).

The line continues on to pass by the slopes of the snow mountain Colquepunku, where one of the most important Andean religious festivals, Qoyllur Riti, currently takes place (Randall 1982:62n6; see also Allen 1988:44) (see Figure 6.1). The festival is considered by many local inhabitants to have primarily involved worship of Ausangate for the fertility of crops and livestock (Flores 1991:234; Gow 1974:80–81; Sallnow 1987:211). Colquepunku is either viewed as part of Ausangate (Gow 1974:57; Sallnow 1987:211, 235) or as deriving its powers from Ausangate (Nuñez del Prado 1969–1970:149). If the line is extended further, it is not far from a pass (and watershed) on which was a ritual site called Walla Walla, where Inca ceremonial offerings were found, including the finest gold statues in Cuzco's Archaeology Museum (Franco 1937:269–276) (Figure A.2). The possibility of the eastern line having been due east is made more likely when the case of the northern line is considered.

Figure A.2. The location of the Inca pilgrimage site of Walla Walla is on a pass near the origin of the Mapocho (later Paucartambo) River. The view is to the southwest with the Ausangate massif in the background.

Zuidema (1986:182, 191–193) has the line to the north actually leading in a northeasterly direction. Although this may be correct for the placement of the ceque lines, if extended farther the line would mean the exclusion of the mountains Sahuasiray and Pitusiray from Antisuyu. Guaman Poma (1956 [1613]:191, 196), however, lists them as among the most sacred places of Antisuyu (Figure A.3). A due-north line would run over Sahuasiray and easily include Pitusiray. They are still worshipped widely in the area today (Sanchez 1984:266), also figuring in a legend in which Sahuasiray provided water to the valley below (Dumezil and Duviols 1974–1976:174). Important ruins lying on or close to the north line include Tambo Machay, Huchoy Cuzco, and Urco (at the foot of Pitusiray). According to Urton (1978:162–164) the north line was established by observing the greatest altitude of the sun at the time of its maximum northern movement.

Thus it would appear that three of the lines may have been along, or very close to, the cardinal directions, at least once extended at a greater distance from Cuzco (Urton 1978:162–164). The line to the south was a different case, however, not being in a cardinal direction but rather having an azimuth of 146°. Zuidema (1982b:98) explains this as attributable to the Southern Cross, along with Alpha and Beta Centaurus, rising in that direction, which also is indicated by the first ceque of Cuntisuyu, called Anahuarque.

Figure A.3. The dark, broken massif of Pitusiray is on the right with the snowcapped peak of Sahuasiray behind it (Mount Chikon is to the left). View is from near Chinchero.

Figure A.4. The layered summit of Huanacauri is on the left and Anahuarque on the right, as seen with a telephoto view from the main street of Avenida del Sol in Cuzco.

Anahuarque was a mountain that played an important role in Inca cosmology, being the only one to save the pre-Inca people in the Cuzco valley when it rose with the waters of a great flood (Zuidema 1982b:97–98). It was worshipped as the ancestress of these people. The peak came to figure prominently in Inca initiation ceremonies, which were also linked with fertility. Along with the mountain Huanacauri, considered one of the most sacred places in the Inca Empire (Cieza 1977 [1553]:105; see also Urton 1990) (Figures A.4 and A.5), Anahuarque was a source of water to a valley that ends near the sites of Wimpillay and Muyuorqo. Wimpillay was occupied by the Wari long before the Incas (Luis Barreda, personal communication 1988), and, in addition to Inca ceramics, Early Horizon pottery (dating to before the time of Christ) was found on Muyuorqo (John Rowe, personal communication 1987). It would seem likely that Anahuarque had an important role in indigenous beliefs prior to the Incas, who then incorporated it into their own conceptual system, the combination of stars and the mountain only taking place when seen from Cuzco.

The point to be made here is that a dualistic symmetry would have required the line to lead due south, but the location of a sacred mountain associated with a

Figure A.5. The author examines ruins on the summit of Huanacauri, considered the second-most-important religious site in the Inca Empire.

water/fertility cult (there is no significant mountain due south of Cuzco), with the added impetus of a link with celestial bodies also associated with fertility, would have been a sound reason for changing the direction of the line. Even then, it is suggestive that important Inca ruins and a rare (for the distance) ritually sculpted rock outcrop lie due south of Cuzco near Pacariqtambo, which eventually became accepted as the place of origin noted in Inca mythology (Urton 1990:29–37) (see Figures 2.4, A.6, and A.7). Zuidema (1988:161) has hypothesized, therefore, that south may have been the cosmological direction of origin for the Incas (and the site built there).

There is general agreement that the western line leads due west. Along this line lie sacred mountains and Inca ceremonial sites such as at Media Luna (Quilla Rumi), Sahuite, and Vilcashuaman (Guchte 1990:190, 228). The first mountain of note is Cerro Tilca, which has Inca ruins on it and has a dominating position above the sacred Apurimac River and the impressive Inca site of Marcahuasi, along with a view toward Salcantay (Angles 1988 (1):1:431, 433–435; see also Heffernan 1996). Continuing on, the equinox line passes near the snowcapped mountain of Ampay. This mountain is believed today to be the dominant deity of the Abancay region (Nuñez del Prado 1969–1970:149). It was likely an important sacred mountain to the Chanka people and for the earlier Wari culture (Anders 1986:784–785, 798), which constructed an important center at Piquillacta (Piquillakta) near Cuzco (McEwan 1987). Since the mountains would already have been worshipped prior to the Inca expansion into the areas they were located, it follows that the mountains were not made sacred by being on the cardinal directions but rather that the directions and mountains combined to add to the sacredness with which they were viewed (see Astete 1990).

It has been argued that there were no terms for "north" and "south" in Quechua, the language of the Incas, but there is evidence that this may reflect a lack of knowledge about how the Incas perceived and named directions and a loss of such terms used by the Inca elite following the Spanish conquest (see Proulx 1988:161 with regard to the term for "south"). To be sure, the cardinal directions may not have been of primary importance relative to other factors, but this is not

Figure A.6. The entrance to one of the buildings at Mauccallakta, which lies due south of Cuzco and is associated by most scholars with Pacariqtambo, a mythical place of origin for the Incas. Bingham believed that Machu Picchu, Pacariqtambo, and Vilcabamba (last capital of the Incas) were one and the same.

147

the same as the opinion of some scholars that they (or at least north and south directions) were not noticed at all. The reason for describing the situation with regard to cardinal directions at Inca Cuzco is because it aids in understanding the importance sacred mountains would have had when found to be in accordance with them, especially the high snowcapped (hence water-providing) peaks as seen from a central place, as in the case of Machu Picchu (Figure A.8).

Figure A.7. A drawing of 1613 shows worship of the mountain Huanacauri, including a symbolic representation of the mythical caves from which the Incas believed their ancestors first emerged at Pacariqtambo (from Guaman Poma 1980 [1613]). Bingham believed that the building he called the Temple of the Three Windows at Machu Picchu represented these caves.

Figure A.8. An aerial view over Machu Picchu and Huayna Picchu.

This photo places Machu Picchu (bottom center) in the context of its mountainous surroundings. The site is located above the Urubamba River near the lower end of a ridge descending from the 6,271 m (20,574ft) summit of Salcantay (upper right, on the back cover). The photo was taken from a pass to the northeast of Machu Picchu. Photo by Octavio Fernandez.

Endnotes

1. Publications devoted exclusively to Inca culture include D'Altroy 2002; Davies 1995; Hemming 1970; Kendall 1973; and McEwan 2006. McIntyre 1975 presents a popular account. See Bauer 1992 for the development of the Inca state; Bauer and Stanish 2001 for the Inca pilgrimage tradition; Hyslop 1984 and 1990 for Inca roads and settlement patterns; Agurto 1987, Gasparini and Margolies 1980, Lee 1985 and 2000, Niles 1999, and Protzen 1993 for Inca architecture; Bauer 1998, Cobo 1990 [1653], Rowe 1979, and Zuidema 1964 for the Cuzco *ceque* system; and Raffino 1981 for an overview of the Inca occupation in the southern part of their empire.

2. For overviews of Inca culture placed within the context of Andean prehistory in general see Davies 1997, Lumbreras 1974, Morris and von Hagen 1993, and Moseley 1992. McEwan (1987 and 2005) discusses the relationship between the Inca and Huari (Wari) cultures in the Cuzco region.

3. The Inca emperor was believed to be in control of the most valuable offerings to the gods and of the religious specialists who made them (see Guaman Poma 1980 [1613]:253). It is likely, however, that other religious specialists would have been involved in making most of the offerings made at regular intervals at Machu Picchu. Those known as *vilca camayos* were in charge of paying homage to the provincial sacred places (*huacas*) and deities (Molina 1959 [1575]:96). They were responsible for establishing the quality and amount of offerings that corresponded to each deity according to its religious importance. *Vilca camayos* would receive the sacrificial victims and offerings brought by the pilgrimage party, and they would be involved in the actual performance of the sacrifices and the burial or burning of the offerings (Molina 1959 [1575]:96). It is likely that priests in Cuzco, and perhaps the emperor himself, determined the amount and quality of offerings made at Machu Picchu.

4. Several accounts of the discovery of Machu Picchu were published by Hiram Bingham (see Bingham 1913, 1915, 1916, 1975, and 1979). His son, Alfred Bingham (1989), wrote a biography of his father that provides additional information of interest. For other publications on Machu Picchu see Burger and Salazar 2004; Frost 1995; Hemming 1981; Kauffmann-Doig 2005; and Wright and Valencia 2001.

5. Cieza de Leon (1977 [1553]:105) listed Huanacauri as second only to the Temple of the Sun in importance. Nuñez del Prado (1969–1970:149–150) describes current-day beliefs about Huanacauri; and Reinhard (n.d.) presents a theory explaining why it became so significant in Inca beliefs.

6. The Apurimac River begins south of the Vilcanota River and roughly parallels it as it flows to the Amazon. It was also considered especially sacred to the Incas, who maintained a major shrine close to it (Cobo 1990 [1653]:108). The chronicler Cieza de Leon (1959 [1553]:151) wrote in the mid-1500s that the fourth-most-important temple in the Inca Empire was Ancocagua (listed immediately after the temple of Vilcanota). We were able to identify this temple in 1994 (Reinhard 1998c). Although it was not constructed at the actual origin of the Apurimac (which, in any event, has several major sources—unlike the obvious, single one for the Vilcanota), it is located on a striking hilltop at a point

where a major ecological transition takes place and agriculture can begin. In a seeming parallel to Machu Picchu and the Vilcanota River to the north, the important center of Choquequirao was built on a ridge overlooking the Apurimac gorge where it is at its most narrow. This is also in the area of transition from the highlands to the lowlands, and the site has striking views to the sacred mountains of the Vilcabamba.

7. Interestingly, although shrines dedicated to Viracocha are fairly rare, there is one near the end of the seventh line of the Cuzco *ceque* system in the quarter of Chinchaysuyu (labeled by Rowe as Ch. 7 and by Zuidema as I1c) (see Bauer 1998:41–42, 168). This line ends as it passes out of sight from Cuzco in the direction of Machu Picchu and is associated with Topa Inca, Pachacuti's son. Farrington (1995:56) shows it extending in a straight line to Machu Picchu. Although there is no historical evidence that the Incas conceptually incorporated more distant sites directly into the Cuzco ceque system, some scholars think this likely (see Zuidema 1982a:439–445). Pachacuti is associated with a line (Ch. 5) close to Ch. 7 that also leads in that direction (see Bauer 1998:58–63, 158).

8. Hiram Bingham (1975:170) noted that the City Gate (or Gateway) was another area with a similarly high percentage of vessels for liquids, and he believed this was due to drinks being offered to people entering there. He stated that this was in contrast to finds made in the southeastern quarter of the site, where food dishes were as common as vessels for liquids. Bingham apparently believed that the offering of liquids at the Gate was only to relieve thirst. Given the sacred nature of the Inca Trail and the sites along it (not to mention Machu Picchu itself), however, it seems more likely that this would have been a place for the ritual drinking and offering of liquids.

This hypothesis is supported by Bingham's discovery of a unique cache of more than 30 water-worn obsidian pebbles near the Gateway. These had to have been brought to Machu Picchu from a great distance, as there had been no recent volcanic activity in the area. They were recently identified as having an origin in the Chivay obsidian source located in the Colca Valley, more than 200 km distant (Burger 2004:104–105). Burger (2004:104) concluded that "it is possible that the obsidian pebbles left at Machu Picchu drew their multivalent symbolic force from their natural associations in the Colca Valley with high mountain peaks, the power of the underworld as manifested by active volcanoes, and the rushing water of the powerful river that shaped this group of unusual translucent stones." Interestingly, Inca ritual offerings have been found on the summits of peaks bordering the Colca Valley (Reinhard 2005). These include the discovery of human sacrifices, called *capacochas*, and are considered the most important of all offerings. To date, however, there have been no finds of human sacrifices having taken place at Machu Picchu or any of its outlying sites.

9. One often hears that the stones used to build the structures at Machu Picchu came from somewhere else. Since the stones would be extremely difficult, if not impossible, to move even with modern machinery, the conclusion reached by some was that advanced technology had to have been involved. The ridge on which Machu Picchu is perched, however, consists largely of granite, which is common throughout the Machu Picchu region (Kalafatovich 1963:218–220). The only rocks thought to be extraneous to the site are small ones that appear to have come from the upper Urubamba Valley, perhaps from Ollantaytambo (Kalafatovich 1963:222). We know from the chroniclers

that the act of quarrying stone would have required offerings to the mountain from which it was extracted (Cobo 1964 [1653]:166, 176).

10. Some scholars have thought that the Intihuatana represented an *usnu* (*ushnu* or *osno*) (Brundage 1967:405; Dearborn and Schreiber 1986:34–35). The term *usnu* has not been easy to define but was usually applied to a stepped pyramid, mound of stones, or a boulder, all of which had a ritual use and were often associated with water (Zuidema 1978:157–162). The more famous usnus are the stepped pyramids at sites such as Huanuco Viejo, Vilcashuaman, and Cuzco (as depicted by Guaman Poma 1956 [1613] vol. 2:30) on which the Inca could sit. But other usnus were noted as being carved rocks on which sacred objects were placed and offerings were made. In this sense of the term the Intihuatana could be interpreted as a type of usnu.

It is suggestive that, when the usnu was made of stones within a ceremonial complex, it was in the shape of a pyramid, which some Andean scholars have interpreted to represent a symbolic mountain (Benson 1972:34, 94–95; Grieder 1982:133; Zuidema and Quispe 1968:30, 32; see also Meddens 1997:11–12). The association with water would be in accord with this, as would the use of the term *usnu* for mounds of stones that, when made in a ritual context, were believed to be places for making offerings to the mountain gods and as symbolically representing them (Ramos 1976 [1621]:68; see also Middendorf 1974 [1895]3:71–72; Reinhard 1988:60–61; Squier 1877:399; Zuidema and Quispe 1968:30, 32). It is also suggestive that the usnu was used as a point from which to observe the sunset by using markers on the horizon (Zuidema 1980:326). The Intihuatana is open to the west, and we have seen how mountains are in alignment with important sunsets as seen from it.

Thus the interpretation of the Intihuatana as representing a mountain would be in agreement with one use of the term *usnu* and suggests, in turn, that the stepped pyramidal platforms used by the Incas were meant to represent symbolic mountains. If this hypothesis is correct, it exemplifies the use of a potent imagery to express the Incas' religious, economic, and political power. It also explains the absence of an usnu platform inside the central plaza at Machu Picchu (Salazar and Burger 2004:348).

11. The other window in the Temple of the Sun (Torreón) provides a view of the sky that includes the tail of Scorpio, which is included in an Inca constellation called Collca (storehouse) (Dearborn and Schreiber 1986:33). This constellation is associated with the storage of crops and is still linked with the planting season in current-day beliefs (see Urton 1981:125).

12. The site should not be confused with Patallacta (also called Llaktapata), a site located at the start of the Inca Trail at Km 88, near the Urubamba River (Kendall 1988).

13. A local trail descends from Llaktapata to meet one that extends along the Santa Teresa River. (A branch of this latter trail ascends to the Inca site of Yurak Rumi.) Bingham had followed a trail from Vitcos that passes by Lake Yanacocha and reaches the Mojon Pass, where it then descends to the Sacsara River. He followed this river until he reached the more heavily traveled Urubamba River trail (Bingham 1916:452–453; 1975:222–223). In 1985 I followed the trail from Vitcos to the Sacsara River, but I found another trail that led from the river through Tambohuayco over a ridge and descended to the Santa Teresa River. Thus, the Incas had at their disposal a shorter,

high route from Machu Picchu that led directly to Vitcos. When the trail was cleared, a fit, unburdened Inca could have covered this route in one long day.

14. For recent studies undertaken with the Bingham collection see Burger and Salazar (2003 and 2004). With regard to estates, Ramírez (2005:250n79) has questioned their origins, and Kauffmann (2005:62) doubts that Machu Picchu could be considered an "estate," noting the different sites along the Inca Trail. For examples of the variety among "estates" see Niles (1999 and 2004). Hyslop (1990:300) provides a summary of the differences between estates and other types of Inca state settlements.

15. Some writers have referred to items found at Machu Picchu that date to after the Spanish conquest. In only two of the 107 burial caves investigated by members of Bingham's expedition were such items found (Eaton 1916:96). In one case a piece of rusty iron was uncovered, which Eaton (1916:79) thought was likely left by a treasure hunter. The other case involved a piece of bovine tibia. Eaton (1916:57) believed that it indicated a burial that took place after the Spaniards arrived, whereas Bingham (1975:198–199) thought that, since no items of commercial value were found at this grave or ones near it, the bone was probably left by a treasure hunter.

Rowe (1990:142) thought it highly probable that the Spaniard Gabriel Xuárez had visited Machu Picchu in the 1560s, when he was one of the early owners of land that included it. The Peruvian archaeologist Julio Tello reportedly found a piece of Spanish alabaster while excavating at Machu Picchu (see Waisbard 1979:133n1), but this, along with any other occasional find, can be explained as either having been left by treasure hunters or brought in by people who occasionally visited the area after Machu Picchu had been abandoned.

There is no solid evidence of a continued occupation of Machu Picchu by the Incas after the Spanish conquest. The presence of Incas living in the region below Machu Picchu noted above does not necessarily mean the site itself was occupied (although occasional visits to it might explain some of the few post-Hispanic artifacts found). Even if this was so, there would have been only a very small population there, and the earlier religious-political-economic activities would have been considerably curtailed, if they continued to exist in any form at all.

16. The most important Inca offering assemblage appears to have consisted of figurines in gold, silver, and *Spondylus* shell representing anthropomorphic beings and camelids (mainly llamas). The anthropomorphic beings would have been dressed in miniature textiles. Other offerings included ceramics (often in pairs and in miniature), objects of metal (such as shawl pins and laminas), bone artifacts (such as tubes or adornments), wooden items (such as vases and spoons), vegetable food items (such as maize and peanuts), and sacrificed animals, usually camelids. In exceptional cases a child (finely dressed with a feathered headdress and a necklace or a bracelet) might be sacrificed (see Reinhard 1985a, 1992a, 2005; Reinhard and Ceruti 2000, 2006, n.d.).

References

1. Garcilaso 1966 [1609]:124.
2. Reinhard 1985b, 1987, 1988, 1990a, 1992d, and 2002.
3. Arriaga 1968 [1621]; Avila 1975 [1608]; Cieza 1959; Cobo 1983 [1653], 1990 [1653]; Duviols 1967; Guaman Poma 1980 [1613]; Ramos 1976 [1621]; Salomon and Urioste 1991.
4. Cf. Hemming 1982:131, 143–150; Kendall 1988:474.
5. Rowe 1979:42–43, 50–51; Valcárcel 1979:20.
6. Pardo 1957:2:458.
7. Angel Callañaupa, personal communication 1986.
8. Nuñez del Prado 1983:158; cf. Marzal 1971:251.
9. See Casaverde 1970:216; Gow and Condori 1982:43; Nuñez del Prado 1969–70:145–146; Rozas 1983:155.
10. See Poole 1984:223; Wagner 1978:55.
11. See Caceres 1988; Contreras 1976; Gow and Condori 1982.
12. Nuñez del Prado 1969–70:146; 1983:158.
13. Quoted in Duviols 1967:28.
14. Santa Cruz Pachacuti 1968 [1571]:293.
15. Marzal 1983:218.
16. Caceres 1988.
17. Middendorf 1974 [1895]:3:412.
18. Waisbard 1979:17.
19. Caceres 1988:67; Luciano Carbajal, personal communication 1989.
20. Washington Rozas, personal communication 1985.
21. Nuñez del Prado 1983:155.
22. Aristibis Cabrera, personal communication 1985.
23. Washington Rozas, personal communication 1988.
24. Guaman Poma 1956 [1613]:196.
25. Duviols 1967:28.
26. Washington Rozas, personal communication 1988.
27. Aranguren 1975:114.
28. See, e.g., Cieza 1977 [1553]:107; Duviols 1967:21, 30; Guaman Poma 1956 [1613]:196.
29. Sanchez 1984:266.
30. Sanchez 1984:266.
31. Wagner 1978:125.
32. See Waisbard 1979:171–173, 292.
33. MacLean 1986:115.
34. See Rowe 1987:16.
35. Rowe 1987:16.
36. Wagner 1978:5.
37. White 1984–85:135.

38. Gary Urton, personal communication 1989.

39. See Zuidema and Urton 1976.

40. Urton 1978:158–160.

41. Urton 1978:160–164.

42. Zuidema 1982b:90.

43. See Avila 1975 [1608]:124–125; Zuidema 1982b:90.

44. Urton 1981:187.

45. Flores 1988:249.

46. Aristibis Cabrera, personal communication 1985.

47. Palomino 1984:32.

48. Urton 1981:174.

49. Urton 1981:70.

50. Avila 1975 [1608]:47.

51. Casaverde 1970:143.

52. Carrion 1955:130.

53. Urton 1981:108.

54. Reinhard 1990a:171–172.

55. Reinhard 1985a:311; Morote 1956:295.

56. Urton 1981:181.

57. La Barre 1948:179, 182–183.

58. Cayon 1971:156.

59. Urton 1981:179.

60. See Urton 1986:46.

61. Urton 1986:60.

62. See Isbell 1978:59, 138, 144; Urton 1986:60.

63. Zuidema 1982b:90.

64. Zuidema 1982b:90–91; Venero 1987:24.

65. Urton 1981:185.

66. Urton 1981:184.

67. Isbell 1978:207; Santa Cruz Pachacuti 1968 [1571].

68. Urton 1981:184.

69. Urton 1978:165.

70. Stuart White, personal communication 1989; see also Morote 1956:295.

71. See Lee 1985:31–32, 41–42; White 1984–85.

72. White 1984–85:134–135.

73. White 1984–85:135.

74. Zuidema 1982a:440.

75. White 1984–85:143.

76. Urton 1981:54; Silverman-Proust 1988:223.

77. Aveni 1980:41.

78. David Dearborn, personal communication 1989.

79. Rowe 1987:16.

80. Bingham 1979:55–57.

81. Bertonio 1984 [1612]:386; cf. Zuidema 1982a:439.

82. Guaman Poma 1956 [1613]:168.

83. Robert Randall, personal communication 1989.

84. Luciano Carbajal, personal communication 1989.

85. Gow and Condori 1982:7.

86. Wiener 1880:349.

87. Ansion 1987:141.

88. Reinhard 1985a:309.

89. Luciano Carbajal, personal communication 1989.

90. Roel 1966:27.

91. Fernando Astete, personal communication 1988; Bingham 1916:449.

92. Fernando Astete, personal communication 1989.

93. Reinhard 1985a:307–309, 314.

94. Szeminski and Ansion 1982:194.

95. Bastien 1978.

96. Gisbert 1980:24.

97. Favre 1967:139–140.

98. Wagner 1978:75, 97.

99. See Avila 1975 [1608]; Duviols 1967.

100. See Agustinos 1918 [1557]:35; and Avila 1975 [1608]:102–105 for prehispanic beliefs; see Marzal 1971:251; Roel 1966:26 for present-day beliefs in the Cuzco region.

101. See Reinhard 1985a:314.

102. Reinhard 1985a:311.

103. Casaverde 1970:146; Gow and Condori 1982:45; Roel 1966:27.

104. Avila 1975 [1608]:66; Cuentas 1982:56; Duviols 1974–1976:279.

105. See Kendall 1988:473.; Cobo 1964 [1653]:175.

106. Martínez 1976:269; Palomino 1984:85; Tschopik 1951:199.

107. Poole 1984:216; Roel 1966:26.

108. Flores 1988:249.

109. Duviols 1974–1976:282.

110. Allen and Albo 1972:59; Nachtigall 1966:374.

111. Cobo 1964 [1653]:80.

112. Bingham 1913:542; Robert Randall, personal communication 1990.

113. Cobo 1964 [1653]:166; see also Ansion 1987:119; Casaverde 1970:142; Favre 1967:138.

114. Caceres 1988:75; Nuñez del Prado 1983; Rozas 1983.

115. Guaman Poma 1956 [1613]:201

116. Middendorf 1974 [1895]:412.

117. Wavrin 1961:144–148.

118. Betanzos 1968 [1551–1557]:13; cf. Roel 1966:26.

119. See Bingham 1979:21, 23.

120. See Beorchia 1985; Reinhard 1993, 1999a, 2005; Reinhard and Ceruti 2000 and n.d.; see also Astete and Reinhard 2003 for Pachatusan.

121. Reinhard 2005.

122. Bingham 1979:48.

123. Cobo 1964 [1653]:169–186; see also Sherbondy 1982:99–101.

124. Sherbondy 1982:144.

125. Ansion 1987:140.

126. Sherbondy 1982; Wright and Valencia 2000.

127. Urton 1981:69.

128. Urton 1981:68.

129. Urton 1981:62, 70.

130. Urton 1981:64.

131. Bertonio 1984 [1612]:386; Zuidema 1982a:439.

132. Urton 1981:64.

133. Gow and Condori 1982:60.

134. Sanchez 1984:267; cf. Isbell 1978:43.

135. Sallnow 1987:129

136. Cf. Squier 1877:400–401.

137. Cieza 1977 [1553]:106.

138. See Zuidema 1982a:440.

139. Urton 1981:202.

140. Reinhard 1990a:168.

141. Rowe 1946:316.

142. Molina 1959 [1575]:57.

143. Rostworowski 1983:38–39.

144. See White 1984–85:143.

145. Randall 1987; Reinhard 1985a, 2005; Urton 1981; Zuidema 1982a.

146. Bingham 1979:58.

147. John Hyslop, personal communication 1989.

148. Sherbondy 1982:139.

149. Polo de Ondegardo 1916 [1571]:110.

150. Polo de Ondegardo 1916 [1571]:110.

151. Sherbondy 1982:139.

152. See Reinhard 1985a:307; Valderrama and Escalante 1988:104.

153. See Martínez 1976:301n25; Reinhard 1985a:306.

154. Bingham 1979:63, 66.

155. Bingham 1979:66.

156. See Girault 1988:55; Menzel 1977:54.

157. See Cobo 1964 [1653]:181; Gow and Condori 1982:61.

158. Gow and Condori 1982:7.

159. Cobo 1964 [1653]:161; Duviols 1974–1976:280; Tschopik 1951:195.

160. See Agustinos 1918 [1557]:22; Avila 1975 [1608]:62; Duviols 1974–1976:280; Tschopik 1951:195.

161. Cieza 1977 [1553]:105.

162. Rowe 1979:35.

163. Gow and Condori 1982:13.

164. MacLean 1986:97.

165. Bingham 1979:52.
166. Rowe 1946:328n39; Markham 1856:181.
167. Uhle 1910:330.
168. See Dearborn and Schreiber 1986:34-35; Hawkins 1973:164.
169. See, e.g., Müller 1982:31–32.
170. David Dearborn, personal communication 1989.
171. Robert Randall, personal communication 1989.
172. Silverman-Proust 1988:228.
173. See Rowe 1946:328n39.
174. Guaman Poma 1956 [1613]:185.
175. See, e.g., Angles 1988:3.117.
176. Robert Randall, personal communication 1989.
177. Bingham 1979:87; Dearborn and Schreiber 1986:22.
178. See Dearborn and Schreiber 1986:22–24.
179. Dearborn and Schreiber 1986:24.
180. Gow and Condori 1982:15; Urton 1981:119.
181. John Carlson, personal communication 1989.
182. See Bingham 1979:89.
183. See Bastien 1978:157; Grieder 1982:133. Guchte 1990:194.
184. Waisbard 1979:235.
185. MacLean 1986:40; Waisbard 1979:235.
186. Ansion 1982:245; Palomino 1984:86.
187. Duviols 1986:55.
188. Paz 1988:221; Jean Jacques Decoster, personal communication 1988.
189. Bastien 1978:xix; Reinhard and Sanhueza 1982:23.
190. See Paz 1988:219–221.
191. Astete and Orellana 1988.
192. Dearborn et al 1987.
193. MacLean 1986:113.
194. MacLean 1986:115.
195. Avila 1975 [1608]:46; Isbell 1978:139, 143.
196. Sherbondy 1982:143; Dumezil and Duviols 1974–1976:174.
197. Reinhard 1985a:307–308.
198. Favre 1967:132.
199. Nachtigall 1966:278; Szeminski and Ansion 1982:198.
200. Bingham 1975:170.
201. Wright and Valencia 2000:21–24; see also Cobo 1964 [1653]:169–186; MacLean 1986:123.
202. See Bingham 1913:473; Salazar 2004:47.
203. Verano 2003:114; cf. MacLean 1986:85.
204. Lyon 1984:4; Rowe 1987:16.
205. Rowe 1987:20.
206. Gasparini and Margolies 1980:87–88; see also MacLean 1986:85–86. For the moat see Wright and Valencia 2000:46.

207. See Fejos 1944:60.

208. Fejos 1944:20–28.

209. Fejos 1944:28.

210. MacLean 1986:126.

211. See Reinhard 1985a:303.

212. Fejos 1944:49–51.

213. MacLean 1986:71.

214. See MacLean 1986:104; Robert Randall, personal communication 1989.

215. See Bingham 1975 and 1979 [1930]; Fejos 1944; Kendall 1988; MacLean 1986.

216. See MacLean 1986:104.

217. MacLean 1986:125.

218. See MacLean 1986:34.

219. Leoncio Vera, personal communication 1989.

220. Arriaga 1968 [1621]:119.

221. David Dearborn, personal communication 1989.

222. Bingham 1975:141.

223. Malville, Thomson, and Ziegler 2004a, 2004b; see also Drew 1984.

224. Reinhard 1990b.

225. Kendall 1988:472; cf. Bingham 1975:142.

226. Bingham 1975:142.

227. Bingham 1975 and 1979 [1930]; Kendall 1988; MacLean 1986.

228. Angles 1988:3:58; Bingham 1979:233.

229. Kendall 1988:462; White 1984–85:136.

230. Berger et al. 1988.

231. See Kendall 1988:473; Rowe 1987:16; Valcárcel 1979:26.

232. Rowe 1987; republished with original text in Rowe 1990.

233. Cobo 1964 [1653]:79; see also Rowe 1946:206.

234. Betanzos 1968 [1551–1557].

235. Rowe 1979.

236. Gow 1974:56–57.

237. Sherbondy 1982.

238. See Beorchia 1985; Duviols 1967; Reinhard 1985a, 2005.

239. Rowe 1987:16.

240. Kendall 1988:474.

241. MacLean 1986:129.

242. Cobo 1964 [1653]:79.

243. Rowe 1987:16, 1990:143.

244. Cobo 1964 [1653]:160.

245. See Agustinos 1918 [1557]; Avila 1975 [1608].

246. Marzal 1971:251; Roel 1966:26.

247. Reinhard 1985b:408.

248. Rowe 1987:16.

249. Rostworowski 1983:138.

250. See Eaton 1916:94–95.

251. See Bingham 1989:351; Verano 2003:81–84

252. Bingham 1989:351.

253. Bingham 1979:233.

254. Hemming 1970:492–499; Lee 1985:25–26, 47–48.

255. See Kendall 1988:472.

256. Waisbard 1979:134.

257. MacLean 1986:129; Rowe 1987:16, 1990:142.

258. Bingham 1916:471; Kauffmann-Doig 2005:63; MacLean 1986:129–130.

259. Gasparini and Margolies 1980:89.

260. Bingham 1916:471.

261. Eliade 1963:99 100; see also Valcárcel 1979:51.

262. Agustinos 1918 [1557]; Avila 1975 [1608]; Duviols 1967; see also Reinhard 1985b, 1988, and 1990a.

263. See Anders 1986; Reinhard 1990a.

264. Randall 1987:82; Sherbondy 1982:144.

265. Randall 1987.

266. See Reinhard 1985b, 1988, and 1990a.

Bibliography

Agurto, Santiago
1987 *Estudios Acerca de la Construcción, Arquitectura, y Planeamiento Incas*. Cámara Peruana de la Construcción, Lima.

Agustinos
1918 [1557]   Relación de la Religión y Ritos del Perú. In *Colección de Libros y Documentos Referentes a la Historia del Perú*, edited by H. Urteaga, 2:3–56. San Marti y Cia, Lima.

Allen, Catherine
1988 *The Hold Life Has*. Smithsonian Institution Press, Washington, D.C.

Allen, Guillermo, and Javier Albo
1972 Costumbres y Ritos Aymaras en la Zona Rural de Achacachi (Bolivia). *Allpanchis* 4:43–68.

Anders, Martha
1986 Dual Organization and Calendars Inferred from the Planned Site of Azangaro—Wari Administrative Strategies. Ph.D. dissertation, Cornell University, Ithaca, New York.

Angles, Victor
1988 *Historia del Cusco Incaico*. 3 vols. V. Angles, Lima.

Ansion, Juan
1982 Verdad y Engaño en Mitos Ayacuchanos. *Allpanchis* 20:237–252.
1987 *Desde el Rincón de los Muertos*. Gredes, Lima.

Aranguren, Angélica
1975 Las Creencias y Ritos Mágicos-religiosos de los Pastores Puneños. *Allpanchis* 8:103–132.

Arriaga, José de
1968 [1621]   *The Extirpation of Idolatry in Peru*. University Press of Kentucky, Lexington.

Ashmore, Wendy, and Bernard Knapp (eds.)
1999 *Archaeologies of Landscape*. Blackwell, Oxford.

Astete, Fernando
1990 Informe de los Trabajos de Excavación Arqueológica del Proyecto de Investigación "Viscacha" Machu Picchu. Instituto Nacional de Cultura, Cuzco.

Astete, Fernando (comp.)
2005 *Catálogo del Museo de Sitio Manuel Chávez Ballón Machu Picchu*. Dirección del Parque Arqueológico Nacional de Machupicchu, Cuzco.

Astete, Fernando, and Rubén Orellana
   1988 Informe Final 1987: Restauración Andenes Mandor Putukusi y Aledaños—
         Machupicchu. Instituto Nacional de Cultura, Cuzco.

Astete, Fernando, and Johan Reinhard
   2003 Investigaciones Arqueológicas Paukarchancha-Pachatusan (San Salvador—Calca).
         Ms. Instituto Nacional de Cultura, Cuzco.

Aveni, Anthony
   1980 *Skywatchers of Ancient Mexico*. University of Texas Press, Austin.

Avila, Franciso de
   1975 [1608] *Dioses y Hombres de Huarochirí*. 2nd ed. Siglo Veintiuno Editores, México
         City.

Barrionuevo, Alfonsina
   2000 *Poder en los Andes: La Fuerza de los Cerros*. Gráfica Bellido, Lima.

Bastien, Joseph
   1978 *Mountain of the Condor: Metaphor and Ritual in an Andean Ayllu*. West Publishing,
         New York.

Bauer, Brian
   1992 *Avances en Arqueología Andina*. Centro de Estudios Regionales Andinos, Cusco.
   1998 *The Sacred Landscape of the Inca. The Cusco Ceque System*. University of Texas Press,
         Austin.

Bauer, Brian, and David Dearborn
   1995 *Astronomy and Empire in the Ancient Andes*. University of Texas Press, Austin.

Bauer, Brian, and Charles Stanish
   2001 *Ritual and Pilgrimage in the Ancient Andes: The Islands of the Sun and the Moon*.
         University of Texas Press, Austin.

Bender, Barbara (ed.)
   1993 *Landscape: Politics and Perspectives*. Berg, Oxford.

Benson, Elizabeth
   1972 *The Mochica*. Praeger, New York.

Beorchia, Antonio
   1985 *El Enigma de los Santuaríos Indígenas de Alta Montaña*. CIADAM, San Juan.

Berger, Rainer, Reinaldo Chohfi, Alfredo Valencia, Wilfredo Yepez, and Octavio
         Fernandez
   1988 Radiocarbon Dating Machu Picchu, Peru. *Antiquity* 62:707–710.

Bertonio, Ludovico
   1984 [1612] *Vocabularío de la Lengua Aymara*. CERES, Cochabamba.

Betanzos, Juan de
   1968 [1551–1557] *Suma y Narración de los Incas*. Ediciones Atlas, Madrid.
   1996 [1551–1557] *Narratives of the Incas*. University of Texas Press, Austin.

Bingham, Alfred
1989 *Portrait of an Explorer.* Iowa State University Press, Ames.

Bingham, Hiram
1913 In the Wonderland of Peru. *National Geographic.* April:387–573.
1915 The Story of Machu Picchu. *National Geographic.* February:172 217.
1916 Further Explorations in the Land of the Incas. *National Geographic.* May:431–473.
1975 *Lost City of the Incas.* Reprinted. Librerias ABC, Lima. Originally published 1948, Duell, Sloan, and Pearce, New York.
1979 *Machu Picchu, a Citadel of the Incas.* Reprinted. Hacker Art Books, New York. Originally published 1930, Yale University Press, New Haven, Connecticut.

Brundage, Burr
1967 *Lords of Cuzco.* University of Oklahoma Press, Norman.

Buechler, Hans, and Judith Buechler
1971 *The Bolivian Aymara.* Holt, Rinehart and Winston, New York.

Burger, Richard
2004 Scientific Insights into Daily Life at Machu Picchu. In *Machu Picchu: Unveiling the Mystery of the Incas,* edited by Richard Burger and Lucy Salazar, 85–106. Yale University Press, New Haven, Connecticut.

Burger, Richard, and Lucy Salazar (eds.)
2003 *The 1912 Yale Peruvian Scientific Expedition Collections from Machu Picchu.* Yale University Press, New Haven, Connecticut.
2004 *Machu Picchu: Unveiling the Mystery of the Incas.* Yale University Press, New Haven, Connecticut.

Caceres, Efraín
1988 *Si Crees, los Apus Te Curen.* Centro de Medicina Andina, Cuzco.

Carmichael, David, Jane Hubert, Brian Reeves, and Audhild Schanche (eds.)
1994 *Sacred Sites, Sacred Places.* Routledge, London.

Carrion, Rebecca
1955 El Culto al Agua en el Antiguo Perú. *Revista del Museo Nacional de Antropología y Arqueología* 11(2):50–140.

Casaverde, Juvenal
1970 El Mundo Sobrenatural en una Comunidad. *Allpanchis* 2:121–243.

Cayon, Edgardo
1971 El Hombre y los Animales en la Cultura Quechua. *Allpanchis* 3:135–162.

Cieza de Leon, Pedro
1959 [1553] *The Incas of Pedro Cieza de León.* Edited by Victor Wolfgang Von Hagen. University of Oklahoma Press, Norman.
1977 [1553] *El Señorío de los Incas.* 2nd ed. Editorial Universo, Lima.

Cobo, Bernabé
1964 [1653]   *Historia del Nuevo Mundo*. Vol. 2. Biblioteca de Autores Españoles, Madrid.
1983 [1653]   *History of the Inca Empire*. Translated and edited by Ronald Hamilton. University of Texas Press, Austin.
1990 [1653]   *Inca Religion and Customs*. Translated and edited by Ronald Hamilton. University of Texas Press, Austin.

Coleman, Simon, and John Elsner
1995 *Pilgrimage: Past and Present in the World Religions*. Harvard University Press, Cambridge, Massachusetts.

Contreras, Jesús
1976 Adivinación, Ansiedad y Cambio Social en Chinchero (Perú). Ph.D. dissertation, University of Barcelona, Barcelona.

Cuentas, Enrique
1982 La Danza "Choqela" y su Contenido Mágico-religioso. *Boletin de Lima* 19:54–70.

Cumes, Carol, and Rómulo Lizárraga
1999 *Journey to Machu Picchu: Spiritual Wisdom from the Andes*. Llewellyn Publications, St. Paul, Minnesota.

D'Altroy, Terence
2002 *The Incas*. Blackwell, Oxford.

Dark, Ken
1995 *Theoretical Archaeology*. Cornell University Press, Ithaca, New York.

Davies, Nigel
1995 *The Incas*. University Press of Colorado, Niwot.
1997 *The Ancient Kingdoms of Peru*. Penguin, Harmondsworth.

Dearborn, David, and Katharina Schreiber
1986 Here Comes the Sun: The Cuzco–Machu Picchu Connection. *Archaeoastronomy* 9(1–4):15–37.

Dearborn, David, Katharina Schreiber, and Raymond White
1987 Intimachay: A December Solstice Observatory. *American Antiquity* 52:346–352.

Drew, David
1984 The Cusichaca Project: Aspects of Archaeological Reconnaissance—The Lucumayo and Santa Teresa Valleys. In *Current Archaeological Projects in the Central Andes: Some Approaches and Results*, edited by Ann Kendall, 345–375. BAR International Series 210, Oxford.

Dumezil, Georges, and Pierre Duviols
1974–1976 Sumaq T'ika: La Princesse du Village sans Eau. *Journal de la Société des Américanistes* 63:15–198.

Duviols, Pierre

1967 Un Inédit de Cristóbal de Albornoz: La Instrucción para Descubrir todas las Guacas del Pirú y sus Camayos y Haciendas. *Journal de la Société des Américanistes* 56(1):7–39.

1974–1976 Une Petite Chronique Retrouvée: Errores, Ritos, Supersticiones y Ceremonias de los Yndias de la Provincia de Chinchaycocha y otros del Perú. *Journal de la Société des Américanistes* 63:275–97.

1986 *Cultura Andina y Represión*. Centro de Estudios Rurales Andinos, Cuzco.

Eaton, George

1916 *The Collection of Osteological Material from Machu Picchu*. Connecticut Academy of Arts and Sciences, New Haven.

Eliade, Mircea

1983 *Patterns in Comparative Religion*. Meridian Books, New York.

Farrington, Ian

1995 The Mummy, Estate, and Palace of Inka Huayna Capac at Quispeguanca. *Tawantinsuyu* 1:55–65.

1998 The Concept of Cusco. *Tawantinsuyu* 5:53–59, Canberra.

Favre, Henri

1967 Tayta Wamani: Le Culte des Montagnes dans le Centre Sud des Andes Peruviennes. *Colloque d'etudes Péruviennes* 61:121–40.

Fejos, Paul

1944 *Archaeological Explorations in the Cordillera Vilcabamba, Southeastern Peru*. Viking New York.

Flores, Jorge

1988 Mitos y Canciones Ceremoniales en Comunidades de Puna. In *Llamichos y Paqocheros: Pastores de Llamas y Alpacas*, edited by Jorge Flores, 237–251. Centro de Estudios Andinos Cuzco, Cuzco.

1991 Taytacha Qoyllurit'i, El Cristo de la Nieve Resplandeciente. *Revista del Museo e Instituto de Arqueología* 24:233–255, Cuzco.

1996 Buscando los Espíritus del Ande: Turismo Místico en el Qosqo. In *La Tradición Andina en Tiempos Modernos*, edited by Hiroyasu Tomoeda and Luis Millones, 9–29. Senri Ethnological Reports 5, National Museum of Ethnology, Osaka.

2004 Contemporary Significance of Machu Picchu. In *Machu Picchu: Unveiling the Mystery of the Incas*, edited by Richard Burger and Lucy Salazar, 109–123. Yale University Press, New Haven, Connecticut.

Franco, José María

1937 Informe sobre Reconocimiento de Restos Arqueológicos en las Cabeceras de Paucartambo. *Revista del Museo Nacional* 6(2):255–277, Lima.

Frost, Peter

1995 *Machu Picchu Historical Sanctuary*. Nueves Imágines, Lima.

2004 Mystery Mountain of the Inca. *National Geographic*. February:66–81.

Garcilaso de la Vega, Inca
1966 [1609]   *The Royal Commentaries of the Inca and General History of Peru*. Part One. University of Texas Press, Austin.
1967 [1609]   *Comentarios Reales de los Incas*. Vol. 1. Colección Autores Peruanos, Lima.

Gasparini, Grazino, and Luise Margolies
1980   *Inca Architecture*. Indiana University Press, Bloomington.

Girault, Luis
1988   *Rituales en las Regiones Andinas de Bolivia y Peru*. CERES, La Paz.

Gisbert, Teresa
1980   *Iconografía y Mitos Indígenas en el Arte*. Gisbert y Cia, La Paz.

Gow, David
1974   Taytacha Qoyllur Rit'i: Rocas y Bailarines, Creencias y Continuidad. *Allpanchis* 7:49–100.

Gow, Rosalind, and Bernabé Condori
1982   *Kay Pacha*. 2nd ed. Centro de Estudios Rurales Andinas, Cusco.

Grieder, Terence
1982   *Origins of Pre-Columbian Art*. University of Texas Press, Austin.

Guaman Poma de Ayala, Felipe
1956 [1613]   *La Nueva Crónica y Buen Gobierno*. 3 vols. Editorial Cultura, Lima.
1980 [1613]   *El Primer Nueva Coronica y Buen Gobierno*. Siglo Veintiuno Editores, Mexico D.F.

Guchte, Maarten van de
1990   Carving the World: Inca Monumental Sculpture and Landscape. Ph.D. dissertation, University of Illinois, Urbana.

Harrison, Regina
1989   *Signs, Songs, and Memory in the Andes*. University of Texas Press, Austin.

Hawkins, Gerald
1973   *Beyond Stonehenge*. Harper and Row, New York.

Heffernan, Ken
1991   Inca Sites in High Places near Cuzco. *Comechingonia* 9:269–299 (número especial). Cordoba (Argentina).
1996   The Mitimaes of Tilka and the Inka Incorporation of Chinchaysuyu. *Tawantinsuyu* 2:23–36.

Hemming, John
1970   *The Conquest of the Incas*. Harcourt Brace Jovanovich, New York.
1981   *Machu Picchu*. Newsweek, New York.
1982   *Monuments of the Incas*. Little, Brown, New York.

Hirsch, Eric, and Michael O'Hanlon (eds.)
1995 *The Anthropology of Landscape: Perspectives on Place and Space*. Clarendon, Oxford.

Hodder, Ian
1999 *The Archaeological Process*. Blackwell, Oxford.

Hyslop, John.
1984 *The Inka Road System*. Academic Press, New York.
1990 *Inka Settlement Planning*. University of Texas Press, Austin.

Isbell, Billie Jean
1978 *To Defend Ourselves: Ecology and Ritual in an Andean Village*. University of Texas Press, Austin.

Jenkins, Elizabeth
1997 *Initiation: A Woman's Spiritual Adventure in the Heart of the Andes*. Putnam, New York.

Johnson, Matthew
1999 *Archaeological Theory*. Blackwell, Oxford.

Kalafatovich, Carlos
1963 Geología de la Ciudadela Incaica de Machupicchu y sus Alrededores. *Revista Universitaria* 121:217–228, Cuzco.

Kauffmann-Doig, Federico
2005 *Machu Picchu: Tesoro Inca*. Editora CARTOLAN, Lima.

Kaupp, Robert von, and Carlos Delgado
2001 Reconocimiento Arqueológico en la Región de Vilcabamba. Ms. Instituto Nacional de Cultura, Cuzco.

Kaupp, Robert von, and Octavio Fernández
1997 Exploración de Sapamarka y Alrededores. Ms. Instituto Nacional de Cultura, Cuzco.
1999 Patrones de Asentamientos Pre-Hispánicos en la Region de Vilcabamba. Ms. Instituto Nacional de Cultura, Cuzco.
2000 Patrones de Asentamientos Pre-Hispánicos en la Región de Vilcabamba. Ms. Instituto Nacional de Cultura, Cuzco.

Kaupp, Robert von, and Lisbeth Rodriguez
2004 Reconocimiento Arqueológico en la Cuenca Norte del Vilcanota. Ms. Instituto Nacional de Cultura, Cuzco.

Kendall, Ann
1973 *Everyday Life of the Incas*. Dorset Press, New York.
1988 Inca Planning North of Cuzco between Anta and Machu Picchu and along the Urubamba Valley. In *Recent Studies in Pre-Colombian Archaeology*, edited by Nicholas Saunders and Olivier de Montmollin, 457–488. BAR International Series 421, Oxford.

Kessel, Juan van

1980 *Holocausto al Progreso: Los Aymaras de Tarapacá*. Center for Latin American Research and Documentation, Amsterdam.

Kolata, Alan, and Carlos Ponce

1992 Tiwanaku: The City at the Center. In *The Ancient Americas: Art from Sacred Landscapes*, edited by Richard Townsend, 317–333. Art Institute of Chicago, Chicago.

La Barre, Weston

1948 *The Aymara Indians of the Lake Titicaca Plateau, Bolivia*. American Anthropological Association, Washington, D.C.

Lee, Vince

1985 *Sixpac Manco: Travels among the Incas*. V. Lee, Wilson, Wyoming.

2000 *Forgotten Vilcabamba*. Sixpac Manco Publications, Wilson, Wyoming.

Lumbreras, Luis

1974 *The Peoples and Cultures of Ancient Peru*. Smithsonian Institution Press, Washington, D.C.

Lyon, Patricia

1984 An Imaginary Frontier: Prehistoric Highland-Lowland Interchange in the Southern Peruvian Andes. In *Networks of the Past: Regional Interaction in Archaeology*, edited by Peter D. Francis, F. J. Kense, and P. G. Duke, 3–18. Archaeological Association of the University of Calgary, Calgary.

MacLean, Margaret

1986 Sacred Land, Sacred Water: Inca Landscape Planning in the Cuzco Area. Ph.D. dissertation, University of California, Berkeley.

Malville, McKim, Hugh Thomson, and Gary Ziegler

2004a El Observatorio de Machu Picchu: Redescubrimiento de Llactapata y su Templo Solar. *Revista Andina* 39:11–42.

2004b Machu Picchu's Observatory: The Re-Discovery of Llactapata and Its Sun Temple. Expanded English version of 2004a. www.adventurespecialists.org/llacta.html.

Markham, Clement

1856 *Cuzco: A Journey to the Ancient Capital of Peru*. Chapman and Hall, London.

Martínez, Gabriel

1976 El Sistema de los Uywiris en Isluga. In *Homenaje al Dr. Gustavo Le Paige, SJ*, 255–327. Universidad del Norte, Antofagasta, Chile.

Marzal, Manal

1971 *El Mundo Religioso de Urcos*. Instituto de Pastoral Andina, Cuzco.

1983 *La Transformación Religiosa Peruana*. Pontifica Universidad Católica del Peru, Lima.

McEwan, Gordon F.
1987 *The Middle Horizon in the Valley of Cuzco, Peru.* BAR International Series 372, Oxford.
2006 *The Incas: New Perspectives.* ABC-CLIO Press, Santa Barbara, California.

McEwan, Gordon F. (ed.)
2005 *Pikillacta: The Wari Empire in Cuzco.* University of Iowa Press, Iowa City.

McIntyre, Loren
1975 *The Incredible Incas and Their Timeless Land.* National Geographic Society, Washington, D.C.

Meddens, Frank
1997 Function and Meaning of the Usnu in Late Horizon Peru. *Tawantinsuyu* 3:5–14.

Menzel, Dorothy
1977 *The Archaeology of Ancient Peru and the Work of Max Uhle.* R. H. Lowie Museum of Anthropology, Berkeley, California.

Middendorf, Ernst
1974 [1895] *Peru.* 3 vols. Ediciones UNMSM, Lima.

Miller, George
2003 Food for the Dead, Tools for the Afterlife: Zooarchaeology at Machu Picchu. In *The 1912 Yale Peruvian Scientific Expedition Collections from Machu Picchu*, edited by Richard Burger and Lucy Salazar, 1–63. Yale University Press, New Haven, Connecticut.

Molina, Cristóbal de
1959 [1575] *Ritos y Fábulas de los Incas.* Editorial Futuro, Buenos Aires.

Morote, Efrain
1956 Espíritus de Montes. *Letras* 56–57:288–306.

Morris, Craig, and Adriana von Hagen
1993 *The Inka Empire and Its Andean Origins.* Abbeville Press, New York.

Moseley, Michael
1992 *The Incas and Their Ancestors.* Thames and Hudson, London.

Müller, Rolf
1982 *Sonne, Mond, und Sterne über den Reich der Inka.* Springer Verlag, Berlin.

Nachtigall, Horst
1966 *Indianische Fischer, Feldbauer, und Viehzüchter.* Reimer, Berlin.

Niles, Susan
1992 Inca Architecture and the Sacred Landscape. In *The Ancient Americas: Art from Sacred Landscapes*, edited by Richard Townsend, 347–357. Art Institute of Chicago, Chicago.
1999 *The Shape of Inca History: Narrative and Architecture in an Andean Empire.* University of Iowa Press, Iowa City.

2004   The Nature of Inca Royal Estates. In *Machu Picchu: Unveiling the Mystery of the Incas*, edited by Richard Burger and Lucy Salazar, 49–68. Yale University Press, New Haven, Connecticut.

Nuñez del Prado, Juan Victor
1969–1970   El Mundo Sobrenatural de los Quechuas del Sur del Perú a traves de la Comunidad de Qotobamba. *Revista del Museo Nacional* 36:143–163.
1983   La Iglesia Andina Actual. *Historia y Cultura* 16:147–159.

Palomino, Salvador
1984   *El Sistema de Oposiciones en la Comunidad de Sarhua*. Editorial Pueblo Indio, Lima.

Pardo, Luis
1957   *Historia i Arqueología del Cusco*. Editorial Rosas, Cuzco.

Paz, Percy
1988   Ceremonias y Pinturas Rupestres. In *Lamichos y Paqocheros: Pastores de Llamas y Alpacas*, edited by Jorge Flores, 217–223. Centro de Estudios Andinos Cuzco, Cuzco.

Polo de Ondegardo, Juan
1916 [1571]   *Informaciones Acerca de la Religión y Gobierno de los Incas*. Sanmarti y Cia, Lima.

Ponce, Carlos
1989   *Arqueología de Lukarmata*. Vol.1. Editorial Sui Generis, La Paz.

Poole, Deborah
1984   Ritual-Economic Calendars in Paruro. Ph.D. dissertation, University of Illinois, Urbana.

Programa Machu Picchu
2000   *Recopilación Bibliográfica del Santuario Histórico de Machu Picchu*. PROFONANPE, Lima.

Protzen, Jean-Pierre
1993   *Inca Architecture and Construction at Ollantaytambo*. Oxford University Press, Oxford.

Proulx, Paul
1988   Lexical Coding and Culture Loss: The Case of Quechua. *American Anthropologist* 90(2):423–424.

Raffino, Rodolfo
1981   *Los Incas del Kollasuyu*. Editorial Ramos Americana, La Plata.

Ramírez, Susan
2005   *To Feed and Be Fed: The Cosmological Bases of Authority and Identity in the Andes*. Stanford University Press, Stanford, California.

Ramos, Alonso
1976 [1621]   *Historia de Nuestra Señora de Copacabana.* Editorial Universo, La Paz.

Randall, Robert
1982   Qoyllur Rit'i, an Inca Fiesta of the Pleiades. *Boletín del Instituto Frances de Estudios Andinos* 11(1–2):37–81, Lima.
1987   Del Tiempo y del Río: El Ciclo de la Historia y la Energia en la Cosmología Incaica. *Boletín de Lima* 54:69–95, Lima.

Reindel, Markus
1999   Montañas en el Desierto: La Arquitectura Monumental de la Costa Norte del Perú como Reflejo de Cambios Sociales de las Civilizaciones Prehispánicas. *Schweizerische Amerikanisten-Gesellschaft Bulletin* 63:137–148.

Reinhard, Johan
1985a Sacred Mountains: An Ethno-Archaeological Study of High Andean Ruins. *Mountain Research and Development* 5(4):299–317.
1985b Chavin and Tiahuanaco: A New Look at Two Andean Ceremonial Centers. *National Geographic Research* 1(3):395–422.
1987   Chavín y Tiahuanaco. *Boletín de Lima* 50:29–49, Lima.
1988   *The Nazca Lines: A New Perspective on Their Origin and Meaning.* 4th ed. Los Pinos, Lima.
1990a Tiahuanaco, Sacred Center of the Andes. In *A Cultural Guide to Bolivia*, edited by Peter McFarren, 151–181. Fundación Cultural Quipus, La Paz.
1990b Informe sobre una Sección del Camino Inca y las Ruinas en la Cresta que Baja del Nevado de Tucarhuay entre los Ríos Aobamba y Santa Teresa. *Revista Sacsahuaman* 3:163–188, Cuzco.
1992a An Archaeological Investigation of Inca Ceremonial Platforms on the Volcano Copiapo, Central Chile. In *Pre-Colombian Art and Archaeology*, edited by N. Saunders, 45–172. Oxbow Books, Oxford.
1992b Underwater Archaeological Research in Lake Titicaca, Bolivia. In *Contributions to New World Archaeology*, edited by Nicholas Saunders, 117–143. Oxbow Books, Oxford.
1992c Sacred Peaks of the Andes. *National Geographic.* March:84–111.
1992d Tiwanaku: Ensayo sobre su Cosmovisión. *Revista Pumapunku* 2:8–66, La Paz.
1993   Llullaillaco: An Investigation of the World's Highest Archaeological Site. *Latin American Indian Languages Journal* 9(1):31–54.
1995   House of the Sun: The Inca Temple of Vilcanota. *Latin American Antiquity* 6(4):340–349.
1996   Peru's Ice Maidens. *National Geographic.* June:62–81.
1997   Sharp Eyes of Science Probe the Mummies of Peru. *National Geographic.* January:36–43.
1998a *Discovering the Inca Ice Maiden.* National Geographic Society, Washington, D.C.
1998b New Inca Mummies. *National Geographic.* July:128–135.
1998c The Temple of Blindness: An Investigation of the Inca Shrine of Ancocagua. *Andean Past* 5:89–108.

1999a Frozen in Time. *National Geographic*. November:36–55.

1999b Coropuna: Lost Mountain Temple of the Incas. *South American Explorers Journal* 58:5, 26–30.

2002 Sacred Landscape and Prehistoric Cultures of the Andes. In *Extreme Landscape: The Lure of Mountain Spaces*, edited by Bernadette MacDonald, 206–225. National Geographic Society, Washington, D.C.

2005 *The Ice Maiden: Inca Mummies, Mountain Gods, and Sacred Sites in the Andes*. National Geographic Society, Washington, D.C.

n.d. Huanacauri, Sacred Mountain of Inca Royalty. Ms.

Reinhard, Johan, and Constanza Ceruti

2000 *Investigaciones Arqueológicas en el Volcán Llullaillaco*. Ediciones Universidad Católica de Salta, Salta.

2005 Rescue Archaeology of the Inca Mummy on Mount Quehuar, Argentina. In *Proceedings of the Fifth World Mummy Congress*, edited by Emma Massa, 303–307. Università di Torino, Torino, Italy.

2006 Sacred Mountains, Ceremonial Sites, and Human Sacrifice among the Incas. *Archaeoastronomy* 19:1–43.

n.d. *The Inca Ceremonial Center on Mount Llullaillaco: A Study of the World's Highest Archaeological Site*. (in preparation)

Reinhard, Johan, and Julio Sanhueza,

1982 Expedición Arqueológica al Altiplano de Tarapacá y sus Cumbres. *Revista de la Corporación para el Desarrollo de la Ciencia* 2(2):17–42, Santiago.

Rendon, Maximiliano

1960 *Cuentos y Leyendas del Valle Sagrado de los Incas*. Editorial Garcilazo, Cuzco.

Riviere, Gilles

1982 Sabaya: Structures Socio-Economiques et Representations Symboliques dans le Carangas-Bolivie. Ph.D. dissertation, Ecole des Hautes Etudes, Paris.

Roel, Josefath

1966 Creencias y Prácticas Religiosas en la Provincia de Chumbivilcas. *Historia y Cultura* 1:25–32, Lima.

Rostworowski, María

1983 *Estructuras Andinas del Poder*. Instituto de Estudios Peruanos, Lima.

Rowe, John

1946 Inca Culture at the Time of the Spanish Conquest. In *Handbook of South American Indians*. Vol. 2, *The Andean Civilizations*, edited by Julian H. Steward, 183–330. Smithsonian Institution, Washington, D.C.

1967 Form and Meaning in Chavin Art. In *Peruvian Archaeology: Selected Readings*, edited by John Rowe and Dorothy Menzel, 72–103. Peek Publications, Palo Alto, California.

1979 An Account of the Shrines of Ancient Cuzco. *Ñawpa Pacha* 17:1–80.

1987 Machu Pijchu a la Luz de los Documentos del Siglo XVI. *Kuntur* 4:12–20, Lima.

1990 Machu Pijchu a la luz de los Documentos del Siglo XVI. *Histórica* 14(1):139–154, Lima.

Rozas, Washington
1983 Los Paqo en Q'ero. In *Q'ero: El Ultimo Ayllu Inka*, edited by Jorge Flores and Juan Nuñez del Prado, 143–157. Centro de Estudios Andinos Cuzco, Cuzco.

Salazar, Lucy
2004 Machu Picchu: Mysterious Royal Estate in the Cloud Forest. In *Machu Picchu: Unveiling the Mystery of the Incas*, edited by Richard Burger and Lucy Salazar, 21–47. Yale University Press, New Haven, Connecticut.

Salazar, Lucy, and Richard Burger
2004 Lifestyles of the Rich and Famous: Luxury and Daily Life in the Households of Machu Picchu's Elite. In *Palaces of the Ancient New World*, edited by Susan Evans and Joanne Pillsbury, 325–357. Dumbarton Oaks, Washington, D.C.

Sallnow, Michael
1987 *Pilgrims of the Andes*. Smithsonian Institution Press, Washington, D.C.

Salomon, Frank, and Jorge Urioste
1991 *The Huarochiri Manuscript*. University of Texas Press, Austin.

Sanchez, Jorge
1984 La Coca en las Relaciónes Inter-ecológicas. *Revista del Museo e Instituto de Arqueología* 23:261–269, Cuzco.

Sánchez, Marino
1989 *De las Sacerdotisas, Brujas y Adivinas de Machu Picchu*. Editora Cotentel Peru, Lima.

Santa Cruz Pachacuti, Juan de
1968 [1571] *Relación de Antigüedades deste reyno del Perú*. Biblioteca de Autores Españoles, Madrid.

Sarmiento de Gamboa, Pedro
1999 [1572] *History of the Incas*. Dover, Mineola, New York.

Shanks, Michael, and Ian Hodder
1998 Processual, Postprocessual, and Interpretative Archaeologies. In *Reader in Archaeological Theory: Post-Processual and Cognitive Approaches*, edited by David Whitley, 69–95. Routledge, London.

Sherbondy, Jeannette
1982 The Canal Systems of Hanan Cuzco. Ph.D. dissertation, University of Illinois, Urbana.

Silverman-Proust, Gail
1988 Weaving Technique and the Registration of Knowledge in the Cuzco Area of Peru. *Journal of Latin American Lore* 14(2):207–241.

Soldi, Ana María

1980   El Agua en el Pensamiento Andino. *Boletín de Lima* 6: 21–27.

Squier, George

1877   *Peru: Incidents of Travel and Exploration in the Land of the Incas*. Harper and Brothers, New York.

Szeminski, Jan, and Juan Ansion

1982   Dioses y Hombres de Huamanga. *Allpanchis* 16:187–233.

Tilley, Christopher

1994   *A Phenomenology of Landscape*. Berg, Oxford.

Tschopik, Harry

1951   *The Aymara of Chucuito, Peru, I: Magic*. Anthropological Papers of the American Museum of Natural History, New York.

Ucko, Peter

1994   Foreword. In *Sacred Sites, Sacred Places*, edited by David Carmichael, Jane Hubert, Brian Reeves, and Audhild Schanche, xiii–xxiii. Routledge, London.

Ucko, Peter, and Robert Layton (eds.)

1999   *The Archaeology and Anthropology of Landscape*. Routledge, London.

Uhle, Max

1910   Datos para la Explicación de los Intihuatanas. *Revista Universitaria* 5(1):325–332, Lima.

Urton, Gary

1978   Orientation in Quechua and Incaic Astronomy. *Ethnology* 17(2): 157–167.

1981   *At the Crossroads of the Earth and the Sky*. University of Texas Press, Austin.

1986   Calendrical Cycles and Their Projections in Pacariqtambo, Peru. *Journal of Latin American Lore* 12(1): 45–64.

1990   *The History of a Myth*. University of Texas Press, Austin.

Valcárcel, Luis

1979   *Machu Picchu: El Famoso Monumento Arqueológico del Perú*. 7th ed. Editorial Salesiana, Lima.

Valderrama, Ricardo, and Carmen Escalante

1988   *Del Tata Mallku a la Mama Pacha*. DESCO, Lima.

Valencia, Alfredo

2004   Recent Archaeological Investigations at Machu Picchu. In *Machu Picchu: Unveiling the Mystery of the Incas*, edited by Richard Burger and Lucy Salazar, 71–82. Yale University Press, New Haven, Connecticut.

Valencia, Alfredo, and Arminda Gibaja

1992   *Machu Picchu: La Investigación y Conservación del Monumento Arqueológico después de Hiram Bingham*. Municipalidad de Qosqo, Qosqo.

Venero, José
1987   La Fauna y el Hombre Andino. *Documento de Trabajo #8*, Proyecto FAO, Cuzco.

Verano, John
2003   Human Skeletal Remains from Machu Picchu: A Reexamination of the Yale Peabody Museum's Collections. In *The 1912 Yale Peruvian Scientific Expedition Collections from Machu Picchu*, edited by Richard Burger and Lucy Salazar, 65–117. Yale University Press, New Haven, Connecticut.

Wachtel, Nathan
1973   *Sociedad e Ideología*. Instituto de Estudios Peruanos, Lima.

Wagner, Catherine
1978   Coca, Chicha and Trago: Private and Community Rituals in a Quechua Community. Ph.D. dissertation, University of Illinois, Urbana.

Waisbard, Simone
1979   *The Mysteries of Machu Picchu*. Avon, New York.

Wavrin, Marquis de
1961   Wayna Picchu. *Revista del Museo e Instituto Arqueológico* 19:136–153, Cuzco.

Westerman, James
1998   *The Meaning of Machu Picchu*. Westbridge Publishing, Chicago.

White, Stuart
1984–1985   Preliminary Site Survey of the Punkuyoq Range, Southern Peru. *Ñawpa Pacha* 22–23:127–160.

Wiener, Charles
1880   *Pérou et Bolivie*. Librairie Hachette, Paris.

Wilcox, Joan
1999   *Keepers of the Ancient Knowledge: The Mystical World of the Q'ero Indians of Peru*. Element Books, Boston.

Wright, Kenneth, and Alfredo Valencia
2000   *Machu Picchu: A Civil Engineering Marvel*. ASCE Press, Reston, Virginia.

Wright, Ruth, and Alfredo Valencia
2001   *The Machu Picchu Guidebook*. Johnson Books, Boulder, Colorado.

Zapata, Julinho
1998   Los Cerros Sagrados: Panorama del Periodo Formativo en la Cuenca del Vilcanota, Cuzco. *Boletín de Arqueología PUCP* 2:307–336.

Ziegler, Gary
2001   *Beyond Machu Picchu: Exploration and Adventure in Peru's Remote Vilcabamba*. Crestone Press, Westcliffe.

Ziegler, Gary, and McKim Malville
2003   Machu Picchu, Inca Pachacuti's Sacred City: A Multiple Ritual, Ceremonial, and Administrative Center. www.adventurespecialists.org/mapi1.html.

Zuidema, Tom

1964 *The Ceque System of Cusco: The Social Organization of the Capital of the Inca.* E. J. Brill, Leiden.

1978 Shafttombs and the Inca Empire. *Journal of the Steward Anthropological Society* 9(1–2):133–179.

1980 El Ushnu. *Revista de la Universidad Computense* 28(117):317–361, Madrid.

1982a Bureaucracy and Systemic Knowledge in Andean Civilization. In *The Inca and Aztec States, 1400–1800: Anthropology and History*, edited by G. Collier, R. Rosaldo, and J. Wirth, 419–458. Academic Press, New York

1982b The Sidereal Lunar Calendar of the Incas. In *Archaeoastronomy in the New World*, edited by Anthony Aveni, 59–107. Cambridge University Press, Cambridge.

1986 Inka Dynasty and Irrigation. In *Anthropological History of Andean Polities*, edited by John V. Murra, Nathan Wachtel, and Jacques Revel, 177–200. Cambridge University Press, Cambridge.

1988 The Pillar of Cuzco: Which Two Dates of Sunset Did They Define? In *New Directions in American Archaeoastronomy*, edited by Anthony Aveni, 143–169. BAR International Series, Oxford

Zuidema, Tom, and Ulpiano Quispe

1968 Visit to God. *Bijdragen tot de tall, land-en Volkenkunde* 124:22–39.

Zuidema, Tom, and Gary Urton

1976 La constelación de la Llama en los Andes peruanos. *Allpanchis* 9:59–119.

Other Resources

SELECTED WEBSITES

1. A listing of Web sites about the Incas: www.ex.ac.uk/~RDavies/inca/links.html
2. Machu Picchu Resources Page: www.tylwytheg.com/machupit.html
3. Virtual tour of Machu Picchu: www.machupicchu360.com
4. Machu Picchu—Virtual Tour Guide: www.dennisadamsseminars.com/machu -picchu/?
5. Machu Picchu—World Heritage Site: www.wcmc.org.uk/protected_areas/data/wh/ macchu.html
6. The Inca Trail and Machu Picchu: www.raingod.com/angus/Gallery/Photos/ SouthAmerica/Peru/IncaTrail.html
7. The Inka Trail: www.archaeology.org/online/features/peru/inka.html
8. Photographic virtual reality visit to Wiñay Wayna: www.stanford.edu/~johnrick/Inca/ WW/pages/WinayWayna.html
9. Johan Reinhard's personal website: www.johanreinhard.org

SELECTED FILMS

Many films about the Incas include scenes taken at Machu Picchu (e.g., *Inca: Secrets of the Ancestors* [Time/Life TV, 1995]; and *Searching for Lost Worlds: Machu Picchu* [Discovery TV, 1997]). Films that focus on the importance of sacred landscape among the Incas include the following:

1. *Inca Mummies: Secrets of a Lost World* (National Geographic TV, 2002) documents the finds of intact Inca burials near Lima and the author's discoveries of Inca mummies on mountain summits.
2. *Mystery of the Inca Mummy* (National Geographic TV, 1996) is about the author's 1995 expedition to Mount Ampato and laboratory work undertaken with the Inca Ice Maiden.
3. *Ice Mummies* (National Geographic TV, 1999) deals with the author's discoveries on Mount Llullaillaco.
4. *Frozen in Time* (Nova, 1997) is about the author's 1996 expedition to Mount Sara Sara.
5. *Light at the Edge of the World: Sacred Geography* (90th Parallel Productions, 2007) examines concepts about the sacred landscape of the Incas, including Machu Picchu.
6. Digital video footage of Machu Picchu is available from the author: johanreinhard@ hotmail.com.

Glossary

*Word origins are indicated in parentheses: S for Spanish, Q for Quechua, and A for Aymara.

aclla (Q). A woman selected for royal service at a young age, who generally was sequestered in special buildings.

acsu (aqsu) (Q). A dress.

alpaca (Q). Lama paco. A domesticated species of Andean camelid with fine wool.

altiplano (S). The high plateau between the eastern and western ranges of Peru and Bolivia.

altomisayoq (S, Q). The most learned and powerful ritual specialist.

Ampato (A, Q). A mountain in southern Peru.

anti (Q). Eastern forested area.

Antisuyu (Q). The eastern quarter of the Inca Empire.

apacheta (apachita) (Q). Mounds of stones, normally found on high places along a road, which are used ritually.

apu (Q). A traditional nature spirit, often a mountain; frequently used in the Inca period to denote a Lord or person of high authority.

Ausangate (Q). A snowcapped mountain to the east of Cuzco.

awki (Q). A general term for mountain deities in the central Andes.

ayllu (Q). A social group that is usually localized and whose members share a common focus.

Aymara (A). An ethnic and linguistic group that bordered the Quechua-speaking region to the east and south of Cuzco.

cancha (Q). See kancha.

capacocha (Q). An Inca ceremony in which sumptuous offerings were made, including the sacrifice of children.

Capac Raymi (Q). One of the most important of the Inca festivals, which took place at the December solstice.

ceque (zeque) (Q). The word for *line* used here to mean a conceptualized line, such as those that formed the system of lines that radiated out from Cuzco.

ch'alla (A, Q). Offering a libation.

chasquis (Q). Runners who carried messages for the Incas.

chicha (Awarak). A fermented beverage, usually made from maize, called aqha in Quechua.

Chinchaysuyu (Q). The northwestern quarter of the Inca Empire.

chullpa (Q). Funerary tower; burial structure.

chumpi (Q). Handwoven belt.

chuño (Q). Freeze-dried potato.

chuspa (Q). Bag.

collca (qollqa) (Q). A storehouse.

coca (Q). Erythroxylon coca. A plant whose leaves contain a mild stimulant.

coya (Q). The principal wife of the Inca ruler.

cumbi (Q). Very fine weaving.

curandero (S). A traditional healer.

curaca (kuraka) (Q). A traditional leader of a community; an indigenous authority.

despacho (S). A bundle containing ritual offerings to nature spirits; it is usually burnt.

enqa (enqaychu) (Q). A natural object, usually a stone, that resembles a thing it is believed to represent and considered to be a repository of its essence.

guaca (Q). See huaca.

guanaco (Q). Lama guanicoe. The larger species of the two wild camelids of the Andes.

hanan pacha (hanaqpacha) (Q). The world above.

huaca (waka or guaca) (Q). A shrine, sacred place, or object. It might also refer to a meteorological phenomenon (e.g., a rainbow) or a feature of the landscape.

Huanacauri (Q). A mountain near Cuzco considered especially sacred to the Incas.

Huayna Picchu (Q). See Machu Picchu.

ichu (Q). Wild bunch grass.

illa (Q). See enqa.

Illapa (Q). Deity of lightning that the Incas believed controlled weather.

Instituto Nacional de Cultura (INC) (S). National Institute of Culture, a government body whose responsibilities include overseeing the protection of Peru's cultural patrimony.

Inti (Q). The sun; the Sun deity of the Incas.

Inti Raymi (Q). One of the most important of the Inca festivals, which took place at the June solstice.

Intihuatana (Q). A sculpted stone at Machu Picchu. Its name means "hitching post of the sun."

kallanka (Q). A long hall.

kancha (cancha) (Q). An enclosure; a group of buildings around a patio.

kay pacha (Q). This world; the earth, as opposed to the underworld and the sky.

kero (qero) (Q). A vase.

k'intu (Q). An offering of coca leaves.

legua (S). A league, or ca. 3.5 miles (5.57 km).

llacta (llaqta) (Q). Town.

llama (Q). Lama glama. A domesticated species of Andean camelid.

lliclla (Q). Shawl worn by women.

Llullaillaco (Q). A mountain on the border between Argentina and Chile.

Machu Picchu (Q). Inca site. The name is derived from *machu* (older) and *picchu* (peak), referring to a mountain bordering the site to the south. It is in opposition to Huayna Picchu (young peak), which is a lower peak to the north.

Mamacocha (Q). Mother lake, usually referring to the ocean.

marca (Q/A). Village or town.

misa (S). Ritual offerings on a cloth, originally taken from the Spanish word *misa* for the Catholic mass, but also associated with *mesa* (table).

mitimaes (Q). Colonists sent by the Incas.

mullu (Q). Mainly used to designate *Spondylus* seashells.

ñañaca (Q). Head cloth.

Ollantaytambo (Q). A town of Inca origin that lies along the Urubamba River in route to Machu Picchu.

pacarina (paqarina) (Q). A sacred place of origin to a group of people.

pacha (Q). The world; earth; time.

Pachacuti (Q). Inca emperor credited with beginning the expansion of the Inca Empire and the founding of Machu Picchu as one of his royal estates.

Pachamama (Q). Earth Mother.

pago (S). Ritual payment to traditional deities.

pampa (Q). Flat plain.

panaca (panaqa) (Q). Group of direct, royal descendants.

paqo (Q). A ritual specialist.

pirca (Q). A building of stones made without mortar.

Pisac (Q). A town of Inca origin that includes one of the royal estates of the emperor Pachacuti.

Pumasillo (Q). A snowcapped mountain to the west of Machu Picchu.

puna (Q). The high grasslands.

pucara (pukara) (Q). A fortress.

Qoyllur Riti (Rit'i) (Q). A festival in the mountains east of Cuzco.

Quechua (Q). An ethnic and linguistic group that was originally concentrated in central Peru, including the region of Cuzco; the language spoken by the Incas.

quipu (khipu) (Q). A knotted string device for use as a mnemonic aid for keeping records.

Salcantay (Q). A snowcapped mountain to the south of Machu Picchu.

saya (Q). A division into halves.

sierra (S). Mountain range, often referring to the Andean highland region in general.

suyu (Q). A quarter; one of the four parts of the Inca Empire.

Tahuantinsuyu (Tawantinsuyu) (Q). The name used by the Incas for their empire, literally meaning the land of four quarters.

tambo (Q). A way station.

t'inka (Q). A libation in which drops of liquid are flicked into the air.

tinku (Q). Ritual battle; literally an "encounter."

torreón (S). Bastion or turret.

tupu (Q). Shawl pin; its synonym is also used to designate a measure of land.

ukhupacha (Q). The underworld.

uncu (Q). A tunic worn by males.

urco (Q). A mountain; also used to refer to the male gender.

Urubamba (Q). Name of the river that flows by Machu Picchu (called Vilcanota in its upper region). Also the name of a town located in the Sacred Valley.

ushnu (usnu) (Q). A raised, stepped platform used in religious and political contexts by the Incas.

Veronica (S). See Waqaywillka.

Viracocha (Q). The Inca creator deity.

vicuña (Q). Lama vicugna. The smaller of the two wild Andean camelids with exceptionally fine wool.

Vilcanota (Q). The name of a river (see Urubamba) originating to the east of Cuzco and also the name of an important Inca religious site located at its source.

waka (Q). See huaca.

wamani (Q). A term for a mountain deity in the central Andes.

Waqaywillka (Huacay Huilque) (Q). A snowcapped mountain to the east of Machu Picchu, often called by the Spanish name Veronica.

yacolla (Q). A mantle worn my males.

yanantin (Q). A matched pair. Also, the name of a mountain northeast of Machu Picchu.

yunga (Q). Warm region.

Index

About the Author

Johan Reinhard is currently (2007) an Explorer-in-Residence at the National Geographic Society and a Senior Research Fellow at the Mountain Institute, Washington, D.C. Born in Illinois, he undertook undergraduate studies in anthropology at the University of Arizona, before going on to receive his Ph.D. (1974) in anthropology from the University of Vienna, Austria. During the 1960s and 1970s his field research was focused on culture change and religion in Nepal.

Since 1980 he has conducted research in the Andean countries of Peru, Bolivia, Chile, Argentina, and Ecuador. His investigations have focused on Inca ritual sites on mountains and on interpreting the ancient pre-Hispanic ceremonial centers of Machu Picchu, Chavin, Tiahuanaco, and the Nazca Lines (giant desert drawings). In the course of his research on sacred landscape he directed teams that made more than 200 ascents above 16,000 feet and discovered more than 40 high-altitude Inca ritual sites, including the recovery of the Ice Maiden and two other Inca human sacrifices on Mount Ampato (20,700 feet) in 1995. His expeditions in the Andes from 1996 through 1999 led to the discovery of 15 more Inca human sacrifices on six mountains above 18,000 feet, including three perfectly preserved mummies excavated at 22,100 feet on Llullaillaco, the world's highest archaeological site. *Time* selected his finds of frozen Inca mummies in 1995 and 1999 as being among the world's ten most important scientific discoveries for those years.

Dr. Reinhard has more than seventy publications, including six books, and is a member of numerous organizations, including the American Anthropological Association, the Royal Geographical Society, the Institute of Andean Studies, the Explorers Club, the American Alpine Club, and the Institute of Nautical Archaeology. He is a recipient of the 1987 Rolex Award for Enterprise in the field of exploration, and in 1992 he received the Puma de Oro, Bolivia's highest award in the field of archaeology. In 2002 he was awarded the Explorers Medal of the Explorers Club of New York. His most recent book *The Ice Maiden: Inca Mummies, Mountain Gods, and Sacred Sites in the Andes* appeared in 2005. He lives in West Virginia.

Email: johanreinhard@hotmail.com
Website: www.johanreinhard.org